DATE DUE

NOV 0 2 2009	

Nursing America

ALSO BY SANDY BALFOUR

Pretty Girl in Crimson Rose (8)

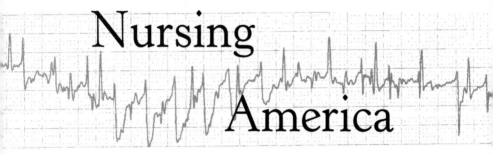

Nursing
America

ONE YEAR BEHIND THE NURSING STATIONS
OF AN INNER-CITY HOSPITAL

Sandy Balfour

JEREMY P. TARCHER/PENGUIN

A MEMBER OF PENGUIN GROUP (USA) INC.

NEW YORK

JEREMY P. TARCHER/PENGUIN
Published by the Penguin Group
www.penguin.com
Penguin Group (USA) Inc., 375 Hudson Street, New York, New York 10014, USA •
Penguin Group (Canada), 10 Alcorn Avenue, Toronto, Ontario, Canada M4V 3B2 (a division
of Pearson Penguin Canada Inc.) • Penguin Books Ltd, 80 Strand, London WC2R 0RL,
England • Penguin Ireland, 25 St Stephen's Green, Dublin 2, Ireland (a division of Penguin
Books Ltd) • Penguin Group (Australia), 250 Camberwell Road, Camberwell, Victoria 3124,
Australia (a division of Pearson Australia Group Pty Ltd) • Penguin Books India Pvt Ltd,
11 Community Centre, Panchsheel Park, New Delhi–110 017, India • Penguin Group (NZ),
Cnr Airborne and Rosedale Roads, Albany, Auckland 1310, New Zealand (a division of Pearson
New Zealand Ltd) • Penguin Books (South Africa) (Pty) Ltd, 24 Sturdee Avenue,
Rosebank, Johannesburg 2196, South Africa

Penguin Books Ltd, Registered Offices: 80 Strand, London WC2R 0RL, England

Library of Congress Cataloging-in-Publication Data

Balfour, Sandy, date.
    Nursing America: one year behind the nursing stations
of an inner-city hospital / Sandy Balfour.
        p.   cm.
    ISBN 1-58542-281-9
        1. Nurses—Tennessee—Memphis—Biography.   2. Nursing—Tennessee—
Memphis.   3. Regional Medical Center at Memphis.   I. Title.
RT34.B34   2005   2004053700
610.73'092'276819—dc22

Printed in the United States of America
10 9 8 7 6 5 4 3 2 1

This book is printed on acid-free paper. ∞

BOOK DESIGN BY BETTY LEW

Most Tarcher/Penguin books are available at special quantity discounts for bulk
purchase for sales promotions, premiums, fund-raising, and educational needs.
Special books or book excerpts also can be created to fit specific needs. For
details, write Penguin Group (USA) Inc. Special Markets, 375 Hudson Street,
New York, NY 10014.

For my mother

Contents

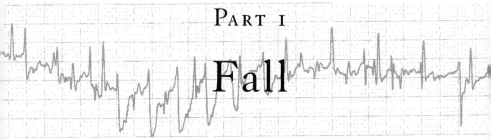

PART I

Fall

CHAPTER 1

All Messed Up in Memphis

"Nobody ever came to the hospital to see a nurse," says Kevin Cox, CRNA. Kevin is a nurse at the Regional Medical Center in Memphis, Tennessee, better known as "the Med." He's thirty-three, broad across the shoulders, with arms to match. Even in his "scrubs"—the loose, pajamalike clothes most nurses at the Med wear—it is easier to imagine him on a building site or rounding up cattle than it is to see him as a nurse. His hair is cropped short and peppered with the first hints of gray, and he has that balance that you develop if you work on your feet for long periods. Beside him stands Lynn Regester, RN. Lynn is older than Kevin, perhaps by fifteen years. He's a nurse anesthetist in the trauma unit and she is a trauma nurse. Being a qualified nurse anesthetist means Kevin is paid considerably more than Lynn. "I'm just a nurse," she says, but in a tone that lets you know she doesn't mean it. In any case, they look and sound like colleagues. They've both been doing "this" for a long time.

It's just after midnight and there is some downtime between

operations. Downtime is unpredictable in a trauma ward. You never quite know what is going to happen next. On this particular evening the kid on the bicycle in Whitehaven has not yet been hit by the car running a red light. The crack cocaine user from "out near Hollywood" has not yet been shot by his dealer. The house in Collierville has not yet caught fire. Everything is quiet. In the trauma wards of the Med they look after patients who are "bent, broke or bleeding," but for one short moment nobody fits that description. Everyone is stable, except they try not to use the word "stable" on the grounds that "the most stable patient of all is a dead one."

Trauma is the most obviously dramatic ward in the hospital. It's here that the kinds of patients that make the evening news are brought. It's here that life-and-death decisions need to be made, and made fast. It can be quiet, but it can be anything but. For Lynn, though, there are advantages. "I like it here," she says, meaning the trauma operating room. "I don't feel I'm on show. I like being anonymous in my mask and gown. I can just get on with my job and do it well. Sometimes we complain that people don't appreciate what we do, but I'm not sure that's always right. Sometimes they do. Sometimes they know we made the difference."

"Sometimes," Kevin agrees, meaning "never." And he tells the story of a patient who came in with his stash of drugs stored in his anus. "A case of 'crack in his crack.' I said, 'What you got in there, man?' And you know what this guy says to me? He says"—and here Kevin is struggling not to giggle—"he says, 'That's some quality stuff, man.'

"Yeah, right," he adds.

But for all that his work involves dealing with various forms of "quality stuff," Kevin (like many nurses at the Med) talks about the Med as "a virus" that gets into your bloodstream and stays there. But he takes it a little further than most. "Working here, one has a certain autonomy, a certain glamour. Other nurses are in awe of you if you work in the OR at the Med. They're, like, 'You really do that?' I like it because I see stuff that I wouldn't see anywhere else.

"But the thing is," Kevin says, "the downside for all of us, all nurses, wherever we work, people come here to see doctors. When people come to a hospital, they ask for a doctor. Nobody ever came to the hospital to see a nurse."

AND YET OFTEN IT IS the nurses they remember. Francee MacLannan has never been a patient at the Med. But her husband

Lynn Regester

has, and she remembers the nurses well. It's July in Memphis and at her neat home in Hernando, Mississippi, Francee is glad to be talking to a writer. A much more eminent local author was once their lawyer, but they haven't seen him for a while, not since he achieved literary fame and fortune. She finds it curious, however, that anyone should choose to write about the Med.

"You're writing about *that* place?" she asks incredulously. "You want to be careful there. I'm worried about you now."

Francee is fifty-something and for most of her life she has been married to Dennis.

"Dennis," she yells. "D'you hear that? He's writing a book about the Med. About the *nurses* at the Med." From the way she says it, it is clear that writing about the nurses is even worse than writing about the hospital. And writing about that hospital is pretty damn bad. Dennis, who until this moment I have not met, comes clumping through from his den. It takes me a moment to register that he is missing his left arm and his left leg is shorn at the ankle, so that he walks on the stump with a pronounced limp.

"The Med, huh? Oh, boy." And he whistles while we shake hands.

"Dennis spent three months at the Med. Didn't you, Dennis?"

"I surely did."

"Tell him what happened."

"Oh, boy," says Dennis with a rueful grin. "He doesn't want to hear all that."

Francee goes all serious now. "Dennis was on the railroads, you know," she says. "He had a job there, but one time he was in an accident."

"A train hit me," said Dennis. "It's a long story."

Dennis tells me the tale of the day he was working in the railroad marshaling yards north of Memphis. "It's where we make sure it all happens right," he says. "You know, so the section with your stuff on really does go to Chicago and not to San Francisco. A lot of stuff comes through Memphis. We're what you might call a crossroad, because we're pretty much in the middle of the country." It's a neat way of describing Memphis, and it tells a lot about the city. The city exists, like St. Louis and Minneapolis, because it is where the great routes west meet the even greater Mississippi River. Dennis tells his story simply and appears not to apportion blame. The accident happened one evening, around six. It was due to a misunderstanding here, an incorrectly followed procedure there. Perhaps if someone had done something different, things wouldn't have happened the way they did. Perhaps if the train had been moving slower, or if Dennis had moved faster—though in truth he didn't have much time to move at all. But Dennis is not really one for "perhaps." He shrugs. "I did all right," he says. "I'm here, ain't I?"

Dennis is remarkably cheerful for a man whose encounter with a train has cost him, literally, an arm and a leg.

"When was this?"

"Nineteen eighty-six," they say in unison. "Nineteen eighty-six."

"So then they called an ambulance and of course the ambulance took him to the Med."

"That's the place they take you if you're all messed up in Memphis," says Dennis. "If anything really bad happens to you around here, you're gonna end up at the Med. It's the only level-one trauma center we've got."

Dennis, too, is fifty-something and he speaks with the broad, beguiling cadences of a native of Mississippi. He has sharp eyes buried in soft features and a mop of unruly hair that he pushes aside from time to time with his remaining hand. You would say of him that he must have been handsome once, and on the wall there are pictures of him as an athlete, playing tennis with the same make of Wilson racket Jimmy Connors used to use. There are a couple of rackets mounted on the wall in his games room. For Dennis, though, those days are past and he spends his time working in the ministry of the small church to which he and Francee belong. Its work has taken them as far afield as Italy, Cuba and Botswana, and Dennis has a canny appreciation that the rest of the world operates on rhythms other than those of Hernando, Mississippi. Francee is not so sure. She still shudders at the thought of the time she spent in Cuba. "I mean the things we were traveling on? Here we wouldn't even call them buses.

"Tell him about the nurses," she says to Dennis.

"Oh, boy," says Dennis. "Those nurses at the Med were awful. I mean, they was rude. They was aggressive. Man!"

"Perhaps things have got better?"

"I don't think so," says Dennis. "Things aren't ever gonna get better at the Med. The Med has been like that for a hundred years. It's gonna be like that a hundred years from now. And I'll tell you why. Because it has to be. The Med has to take anyone who comes to its door, and anyone who comes to its door don't always have the money to pay. And if you aren't paying, you aren't gonna get lots of nurses going all sweet on you. If you aren't paying, they're gonna do what they have to do and then leave you to it."

"You did, Dennis. You paid. You were insured," says Francee.

"Yes, I was. I was insured," repeats Dennis. "I was that, so they did all right out of me for my three months. They got paid plenty for what they did for me."

"The money!" says Francee. "When Dennis was there it cost them, the insurance company, maybe a million dollars. More.

"Two million," she says, by way of illustration.

As an extension of this thought she says that she now pays five hundred and something dollars a month in health insurance premiums that "don't cover half of what I need." She mentions, almost casually, that when Dennis was at the Med the surgeons tried seven times to sew his arm back on. "Seven times! But they couldn't do anything with it. It was just there on the table."

"A million dollars," says Dennis, and he pauses at the memory.

"But there's lots of people who ain't insured. Lots of people," he says, nodding. "And the Med still takes them, same as everybody else."

"And the nurses were rude?"

"Oh, man," says Dennis. "Man, I can't tell you. One of them stepped on my tubes. Just about pulled the whole dang thing out."

"Just terrible," says Francee, fussing in the kitchen. "Just terrible. The way they talked to him. Oh!"

"'Course, they saved my life," says Dennis.

"There was that," Francee concedes. "Those nurses did save your life."

Which is one reason to remember them.

CHAPTER 2

One Choice in Three

MARYE BERNARD, FNP, is one nurse whom people do come to the Med to see. She is the nurse practitioner—a nurse with a master's degree—in the Adult Special Care Unit of the Med, which is a euphemism for the section of the hospital that provides care and support for outpatients with HIV or AIDS. Marye was born forty-three years ago in midtown Memphis and her earliest memories are of walking to the Catholic church not far from Hollywood Avenue. "We had to go past the bakery on the way to church and sometimes if I'd been good and if maybe my granddaddy is visiting, he would take us to the bakery and buy us something. Man! I loved that bakery."

Marye's average day consists of a patient load of perhaps fifteen people, together with phone calls, paperwork, meetings and so on. It's 10 A.M. in Marye's small, cluttered office when she calls a patient to find out how he is doing. He is doing "great," and with another nurse the conversation might have ended there, but Marye knows her patients too well for that.

Slowly, methodically, surely, Marye unpicks his halting testimony to find out what it is that is really bothering him, and why he called in the first place.

"And the diarrhea?" she asks. "It's still there? It is? Well, baby, I know why you've got it. You've got a bacteria, that's what it is, so I'm gonna need to give you some medicine. Now, I know you can't just come in here. I know that, so I'm gonna do it over the phone, okay? Where's your pharmacist?"

She listens while the patient tells her the pharmacy and the address.

"Russell's?" she asks. "Really? Is old man Russell still there? Man! I used to go there as a kid. He's still alive? He must be a hundred and ten years old."

Perhaps being a grandmother at forty makes you feel older than you really are. It's not *that* long since Marye was a kid.

She calls the pharmacy and spends some minutes explaining who she is and what she needs. But Russell's does not have the antibiotic she has in mind and it takes several calls to the patient and to other pharmacies before she finds someone nearby who can fill the prescription that afternoon. While she waits on the line Marye continues to give me thumbnail sketches from her life. She remembers how one time her granddaddy bought her a whole cherry pie, just for her.

"I never forgot that cherry pie," she says, "and I never will. 'Cause we were poor, you know what I'm saying? And to have a whole pie to yourself? Man, that was something!"

Her church—St. Therese in midtown Memphis—integrated early. Marye can remember that the monsignor marched with Martin Luther King, Jr. She remembers it with pride. Some of the confidence and the defiance rubbed off on her. But she remembers also how it felt. Her priest was being arrested on television? It was embarrassing. What would people think?

"Of course," she says, "it being a Catholic church, there were plenty of Irish kids around. I remember there was this one neighbor, a girl the same age as me, and she and I would plait each other's hair. But then her mother stopped us. She didn't want her daughter playing with no black girl's hair.

"Nowadays they find different reasons for their kids not to play with yours. Nowadays they don't want you playing with their daughter if you're HIV positive. Or because you *might* be HIV positive. Or because you once met someone who knew someone who had heard of someone who might have been related to someone who might be HIV positive. . . . You know what I'm saying?"

ADULT SPECIAL CARE is housed on the fifth floor of the Med-Plex building. As people come into the unit to start their day, Marye yells out a greeting to each.

"Hey, how're you doing?"

"Hey yourself," her colleagues reply.

As to the question of how she became a nurse, Marye just laughs. "The decision was made for me," she says. "Back when I left high school, there were three things an African-American girl like me could do. We could be a teacher, be a social worker or become a nurse. And at school my adviser looked at my grades and my 'aptitudes'—you know, like things that interest me or I'm good at—and said I should go to nursing school. And

I was happy with that because in my community teachers were respected, but they were poor. So I didn't want to be a teacher. I wanted to have more money than what you would get as a teacher."

Marye graduated with her master's in nursing from the University of Tennessee and went to work first for the university and then for the Shelby County Health Department. She came to the Med five years ago.

"Back then"—the time when "a girl like Marye" had only three career choices—was not that long ago. She would have turned eighteen in 1975, more than a decade after President Johnson signed the Civil Rights Act into law. And of those three careers, nursing would have been the most difficult to enter. Then as now, places in nursing schools were competitive. Not everyone got in. But Marye did and went on to study for her master's. For a time it looked like a career in academia might appeal—but then she made the move to the Med.

"At first—I'll be crude—I came for the money. But that's not why I'm here now. Now they'd have to drag me out of here. I'm doing what I love, and half the time I'm, like, 'Wow, they pay me to do this.'

"Because these are my people, you know. It's like I'm taking care of family."

Marye is Memphis-born and -bred. "In fact I was born right here at the Med. And my mother was born here, too. Of course, then it was the John Gaston. And you know, my momma always had two birthdays. There was the day she was born and then there was the day my granddaddy paid his hospital bills—which was the day they entered on the birth certificate. Because my granddaddy was a pastor, he didn't get paid until Sunday. Saturday was always a real bad day in the house. No money, not much to eat. So it wasn't until the next Monday after Momma was born that he had the money and that was when he came in to pay the bill. And so that was the date they put to say when my momma was officially born. In fact she was already a few days old. But until he had paid, it was like she didn't exist. Can you imagine that?

"Not much changes, huh," she adds.

Like many African-Americans in Memphis, Marye's association with the Med is long and deep. Generations of the family were born there and several members of the family have worked there. "My auntie Freddie was one of the first African-American nurses hired by this hospital, you know, back when they wore those white uniforms with the starch and the hats and all?"

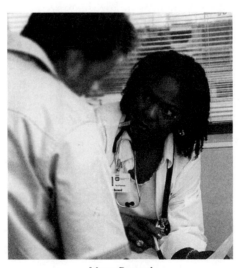

Marye Bernard

I have a book of photographs of nurses from "those times." The uniforms have changed over the years, from the tight Victorian outfits of the late nineteenth century to the loose scrubs of today. In trauma wards it is sometimes hard to tell who is a nurse and who a surgeon. In theory the nurses wear dark blue and the surgeons green. Nursing assistants wear maroon. In practice, however, nurses wear all sorts of scrubs. It depends on who has been bleeding on them recently. And in the labor wards nurses tend to wear softer colors and pastel coats over their scrubs. Marye doesn't wear a nurse's uniform. She has a lab coat on, but otherwise could pass for an administrator or a doctor. But she's not thinking about that. She's still remembering her aunt Freddie, who, like her, was born at the Med.

Chapter 3

✚

Done Treated Right

IT'S NOT HARD to find people in Memphis who were born at the Med. While there are those like Dennis and Francee MacLannan who shudder at the memory of a traumatic experience at the hospital, there are many more for whom the Med is where they were born and where, if they thought about it, they might expect to die.

The hospital itself straddles three or four blocks in the no-man's-land between downtown and midtown. Its architecture reflects its history. Over the years different buildings have been added to or taken away from the Med. There's been a city hospital "there" since 1829. The "Pavilion" on Jefferson Street now houses the administration wing of the hospital, but in its time it has been an "isolation hospital," a children's hospital and a residence for interns and residents. The buildings that house the delivery unit were funded by the French-born philanthropist and restaurateur John Gaston, and developed from the E. H. Crump Hospital for Negroes. They were built in 1956 but had long since been incorporated into the Med. In its 170-year history the hospital has been known successively as Memphis Hospital, Memphis City Hospital, Memphis General Hospital, John Gaston Hospital, City of Memphis Hospital and now Regional Medical Center, Memphis.

Like everyone in Memphis, the woman who runs a coffee stand near Beale Street knows where it is. In fact—like many—she was born there. She's wearing a green baseball cap and a bright blue T-shirt that reads "If Elvis were alive, he'd live in L.A."

"It's my joke," she says. Too many of the foreign tourists who come to Beale Street, the "home of the blues," are interested only in Elvis Presley's former home, Graceland, and she is tired of giving them directions on how to get there.

"Everybody here takes the whole Elvis thing so seriously," she says. "You know what I'm saying? But I'll tell you, money or not, there are folk here who don't think this shirt is funny at all. Mind you, there are folk here who don't think Elvis is dead." And she chuckles at her joke, before coming out from behind her stand to point the way to the Med. "Go up Second," she says, "and take a right on Union. Or better, go right on Madison. It's a couple of miles, so maybe you'll need to take a cab?

"What are y'all doing at the Med, anyways?" the woman asks. "I was born there," she says, and then she shrugs in explanation. "'Course, back then it was the John Gaston. My name's Angela, by the way."

Angela pauses, uncertain whether to continue. She is perhaps forty years old, young enough to have been born during the civil rights struggles and old enough for her parents to have worn the scars of segregation. Her chocolate skin warms to the wintry morning light and complements her yellow anorak. She has a soft, friendly, slightly puffy face and wide eyes, and she wears no makeup. Like many people who work in public places, she has straying eyes that wander across, rather than to, my face from time to time. She's keeping an eye out for customers, but seems to have more to say and I am aware that she is representative of a large swath of the people who come to the Med. For generations of people, mostly poor, from Tennessee, Mississippi and Arkansas, it has been a refuge and salvation and—to a degree—an embarrassment. Public hospitals have a stigma born of generations and to go to the Med for treatment is perceived by some to be an admission—or acceptance—of a certain economic status, or lack of it. If you are a patient at the Med it may well be that you are one of the 40 million or so Americans who do not have any form of health insurance, not even from Medicare, Tenncare or any other publicly sponsored scheme. Or perhaps you are old enough, or young enough, to be covered by Medicaid or Medicare, and are one of the 30 million Americans who therefore, as the statistics say, have "some kind of health coverage." In that case you, too, will more than likely end up at a hospital like the Med. The national average for those who have no coverage at all is 14 percent, but in Tennessee, Arkansas and Mississippi, the three states most served by the Med, the averages are 15 percent, 18 percent and 20 percent, respectively. And in Shelby County, including the city of Memphis, one in four of the population has no medical insurance whatsoever. It is no coincidence, one assumes, that these figures closely match the number of Americans deemed by the federal government to live below the poverty level.

It turns out that Angela is one of those who have no insurance coverage at all.

"Selling coffee? Here? I don't think so," she says.

"Don't employers have to insure you?"

"They do that," she replies. "But I don't have no employer. I'm my own boss, and this here is my coffee stall. And ain't it the best?"

"But don't you have to insure yourself?"

"Oh, sure," she says. "Sure I do, but I can't. Not on what this earns me."

As she tells her story it becomes all too easy to understand how it is that she, and her extended family, come to have no health coverage. For a start there are the numbers. In her household there's her and three daughters, and one of the daughters—the eldest, she's twenty-two—has two kids of her own. So that's, what?—and here Angela counts them off on her fingers—two, four, six people. Then there's her mother and her mother's sister. So that makes eight in her household. Even minimal insurance for those eight—four adults and four minors—comes to just under four thousand dollars a year, and even then there is a several-thousand-dollar excess on any claim.

It just ain't, in Angela's words, worth the candle. "There ain't none of us has that sort of money. I ain't got no money, and I'm the only one that has any money at all."

It is 9 A.M. on a bright day and business on Beale Street is slow. By night the street gives every appearance of being a thriving home to the blues, with each of its many bars and clubs blaring music out into the street. With some justification Beale Street promotes itself as the place where the blues began. The songs and sadness that welled up in the cotton and sugar fields of the Mississippi Delta found their first commercial expression here when W. C. Handy wrote and later published a bluesy campaign theme for the city's new mayor, Edward H. Crump. Crump was later to lend his name to a "hospital for Negroes," which in due course became part of the Med. From its heyday in the forties, Beale Street declined for several decades before being reinvented by the city on the back of a growing appreciation of the blues, both for the music and for the strength of its storytelling. By night the clubs and bars rock with music, even if they are catering largely to the tourist trade.

Angela has one more thing to say.

"Let me tell you something about the Med," she says. "It ain't what we asked for, and it ain't what it could be. But it's what we got. Sometimes they talk, them guys at City Hall or the governor and the like? They talk 'bout closing it down. It costs this, it costs that. You know what I'm saying? Well, they can talk all they want, they won't never close it down. Because it's what we've got. It's all what we've got. It's the place where I was born.

"So you mind you say the right thing. You treat those nurses in that hospital right, you hear, because they done treated me right and I ain't never paid them a dime."

Chapter 4

Older than Time

Spend any time at the Med and sooner or later someone will say to you that "the Med is its nurses" or, sometimes, "the nurses *are* the Med." There are varying justifications. Most prosaically, the nurses make up the bulk of its workforce and the physicians who might otherwise have been thought to "define" the hospital are formally employed by the University of Tennessee and other institutions. Less prosaically, of course, are the emotional associations that patients make with a hospital. Doctors and residents they see only irregularly. For any patient it is the nurses who are the constant and it is the nurses who define the experience of being there.

Dennis MacLannan, who lost an arm and a leg in a train accident, but who survived because of the care he received at the Med, remains unshakable in his conviction that the hospital will never "be a good place to be." The hospital has been "like that" for a hundred years, he told me, and it will, he predicted, be "like that" a hundred years from now. In one sense he may be right. The hospital has "always" catered to the poorest members of its community and continues to do so now. An article written in 1912 for *The Commercial Appeal* (still the largest-circulation daily paper in the mid-South) could as easily have been written today. "The Memphis City Hospital [now the Med] which has so often been a bone of contention in political and medical circles, appears to have fairly [*sic*] settled down, for the time being at least, to the achievement of its normal destiny. Some changes have been made. Some new features added. Some reforms introduced." The article goes on to describe the new recruitment of a corps of trainee nurses who are "provided" to patients able to pay—free if it is an emergency or at a rate of $1.50 (including board) for more routine medical treatment. But the article soon cuts to the chase: "It costs money to run an institution like this. It costs from $5,000 to $6,000 and up a month. . . ." That "and up" is significant. Costs are never entirely predictable because they are driven by demand, and who knows what the demand will be from day to day?

The story is, of course, even older than that. There is evidence that the first hospital in Memphis—or, rather, in the area that was to become Memphis—was part of Fort Ferdinand. It would have been built in 1776, that revolutionary year. Plans of the fort on the bluffs above the Mississippi show a hospital section, and it would have been characteristic of the Spanish to build one. Whether it was any good or not is not clear, but there is evidence that many sick men were sent down the river to receive what one hopes was more adequate medical treatment in New Orleans.

The Med is the successor to the second known hospital in the city. It was shortly after the city was incorporated (in 1826, by a group of lumber merchants and boosters including the future president Andrew Jackson) that the Tennessee legislature appropriated funds to build and then provide an operating budget for what was to become the Med.

In 1829 Memphis had only 700 residents. Curiously, those who lived in the city had no access to the hospital, the point of which was the custodial care (and presumably isolation) of sick travelers. The Mississippi by that time had become a conduit for disease in much the same way, say, as the trucker routes of Africa today have contributed to the rapid spread of HIV throughout the continent. Writing as early as 1834, one commentator was in no doubt as to the malign properties of the river: "Perhaps there is no river in the world, whose waters and borders witness as much sickness and death as the Mississippi. Ambitious, enterprising young men . . . forsake their homes of plenty, parents, brothers and sisters—the very sanctuary of happiness on earth—throw themselves on the bosom of the Ohio in a miserable damp *flat boat,* float into the whirling Mississippi, and haste along its grey turbulent waters, into the region of sickness and death [where] you die, unknown and unwept, and in thoughtless silence buried upon the brink of the river, perhaps without shroud or coffin, a tree or stick for a tomb-stone, a hill of mud swelling over your body, and the first heaving of the mighty river sweeping all away into the recesses of its turgid bowels."

Even now the city has a curiously ambiguous relationship with the river. The wealth it has brought through trade, especially in cotton, now arrives silently by electronic transfer. The tows still steam past. On any day you can sit on the Chickasaw Bluffs and watch them churning their way beneath the Hernando de Soto Bridge—but few stop at Memphis. They are going to more important ports: St. Louis and Baton Rouge, New Orleans and the twin cities of Minneapolis–St. Paul. In Memphis the riverfront, once the center of a vast cotton industry, is now a mix of parkland and residential development. At the bottom of Beale Street, in the backwater created by Mud Island, a few riverboats entice tourists on brief boat trips, but they, too, have a desultory and saddened air. The water in the river is plentiful but it is not fit to drink, nor is it safe for swimming. Drinking water comes instead from abundantly supplied aquifers deep below the river.

The river, like everything else in Memphis, is never quite what it seems, neither as benign, nor as hostile.

NOWADAYS MEMPHIS IS home to a little over 1 million people, but in the nineteenth century it was a small, dirty, muddy town, swept by successive epidemics, particularly of cholera and yellow fever. The purpose of the original hospital was to protect the townsfolk from travelers, rather than to care for its own. In this sense "the hospital was a continuation of the medieval Christian concept of charity that took the form of a hospice—a place for the weary or sick traveller to rest and recover before continuing his journey," which is how it was described in an editorial in *The Randolph Recorder* in September 1834.

From the earliest days the hospital found itself torn between its public service remit and the need to pay for itself, and within five years of its opening the first of many requests for federal funding was sent to Congress in Washington, D.C. For the first but not the last time, Congress ignored this appeal. These sorts of relations have played themselves out time and time again over the years. In 1853, for example, the federal government agreed to pay for the medical care of sick riverboatmen. The report for 1855 shows that 590 patients admitted to the Memphis Hospital had financial support from public funds: 144 from the U.S. government, 132 from the City of Memphis and 314 from the State of Tennessee. Writing in *The Commercial Appeal* 150 years later, Louis Donelson, chairman of the board of the Med, paints a remarkably similar picture. Arguing for further funding from the state, he says the $12.2 million offered by the state is barely adequate. After all, Shelby County provides a steady $31 million per year, and the government pays the state of Tennessee "approximately $50 million in federal matching funds based on the Med's uncompensated care and Tenncare losses." The state, however, has been unwilling to hand this money over to the Med, preferring to divide it between nine "essential access provider hospitals." The Med's share? $12.2 million in the 2002–2003 fiscal year.

The current governor of Tennessee, Phil Bredesen, one of whose responsibilities is the administration of the state's health insurance scheme, Tenncare, is not the first to see the Med as an intractable problem. Tennessee withdrew from the federal Medicaid scheme and replaced it with Tenncare in 1994. "Yes, they need to have Tenncare help . . ." Bredesen is reported as saying of the Med, "but that does not solve their problem. It just postpones it by $3 million or $6 million. . . ." One wonders how the governor, if pressed, would define the problem and why he thinks it is "theirs" rather than "his."

"It's a problem for all of us," agrees Dr. Bruce Steinhauer when I meet him in his office. "The question of who pays for those who cannot pay for themselves. And every generation says that what we need is a permanent solution. But there never is one."

Dr. Steinhauer is CEO of the Med and has been for five years, which means he has easily outlasted his two predecessors. Being chief executive of a place like the Med can take its toll, but on this morning Dr. Steinhauer looks ready for whatever challenge the hospital can throw at him.

"I can explain it," he says, "but it is a very sardonic answer. The reason there is no permanent solution to the question of how we pay for health care in this state—or in the country, for that matter—is that in Nashville there are many people whose only business is to influence health policy. A permanent solution would put them all out of business."

Dr. Steinhauer is a small, dapper man. This morning he is wearing a gray suit, blue shirt and his trademark bow tie. His round steel-rim spectacles give him a professorial air. It is easier to imagine him as an academic than as a hospital administrator. He is calm and gentle. And he has a sharp sense of his own place in the greater scheme of things.

"I would be more effective," he says, "if I came from here. My accent, you know, those flat Midwestern vowels, don't work here. They don't fit." Steinhauer comes from Ohio and is a graduate of Harvard Medical School. "People here expect a certain rhythm of speech. I have to work a lot with what you might call the Tennessee aristocracy and not being native makes me less effective. It would be easier if I had the right syntax. It takes people here longer to figure out what I am saying."

This is not false modesty. It's just a political reality.

The cry of "politics" in the operation of the hospital was raised in the 1850s and this same cry has been raised many times since. "There are two schools of thought with which I have to contend," says Steinhauer. "Everyone agrees that in health care you are always going to have to have a public sector. In the old days it was isolation, you know, of people with infectious diseases and so on. Nowadays we are more progressive than that." He smiles at the thought. "But still people say one of two things. One side says you should pay for it. The other side says that if you starve the public sector, some of its customers will shape up."

And where does he stand?

"There is some truth in both sides. I don't buy this idea of the inherent superiority of the private sector—which often persists in the face of overwhelming evidence to the contrary. But I know that the man in the street thinks this place all costs too much."

And politically where does he stand?

"I was a Republican until I came to Tennessee. Now this hospital is my party."

One consequence of the cry of "politics" was that in 1848 the Med became a teaching hospital, or, as the Tennessee legislature put it, "medical students of the different medical schools in Memphis shall be permitted to visit the hospital under the supervision of the attending physicians."

For the current crop of nurses this is a mixed blessing. Many cite it as one of the great benefits of being a nurse. Because of the relatively high turnover of "residents"—the commonly used term for graduate doctors doing their "residency"—nurses have greater trust and experience. They know that the doctors need them. On the other hand it puts greater strains on the nurses. "July is the worst," one told me, "because that's when all the residents change. You've just got one lot trained and working properly and they all leave and a new lot come in. And you have to start all over again."

But the more important consequence is the air of permanent insecurity. The hospital's financial year runs from July 1 to June 30. As early as the fall, conversations are full of "if they don't close us down" comments. In the absence of a public consensus that there is—even if only de facto—a shared responsibility for poorer people, and in the context of a public discourse focused primarily on the relentless reduction of the tax burden (even when this is not practiced), this insecurity has remained. Strange to tell—but true nonetheless—that in 2002 the debates of the 1830s were being repeated with the same halfhearted "solutions" and the same inevitable talk of "crisis."

Chapter 5

Sister Soldier

BACK AT THE Adult Special Care clinic, Marye Bernard, RN, catches a glimpse of her face in a hallway mirror. She's still talking about her aunt Freddie, who was one of the first black nurses at the Med. "People here have long memories," she says. "When I came here people remembered and they all called me Aunt Freddie. Except the patients. The patients, some of them, they call me Sister Soldier because of how I wear my hair." Marye wears her hair in "locks," which gives her face a rounder, softer feel. Today she's wearing slacks and a pastel blouse, but as usual it's all hidden under her white lab coat.

She has roughly 1,400 patients registered at the Adult Special Care Unit and five days a week, twelve or fourteen of them have an appointment to see her.

"But first I gotta pray," she says, sitting at her desk in the small windowless room that serves as her office. "I gotta get ready for my day." She's listening to a CD from South Africa; the CD itself is a fund-raiser that came out of the World AIDS conference held in Durban on South Africa's east coast. It's a recording of a church choir singing hymns in Zulu.

"You understand that?" Marye asks. "Whatever language they're using? I listen to these songs from all over the world when I'm getting ready in the morning. I like to come in a little early, say my prayers, do my e-mails, get, you know, my spirit ready for the day.

"What I do also," she continues, " is set my personal goals for the day. What I'm going to accomplish, whom I'm going to see. And I pray to God for help with that."

"Which church?"

Marye gives a very specific answer. "We belong to a place out in Covington. It's about thirty-five miles out of town and every Sunday we go out there to worship."

It takes a second question to find out which denomination.

"Baptist," she says. "My mother's family are all from Memphis, but my father comes from Louisiana, so I was raised Catholic. But I converted with my husband and now we go to this special place in Covington."

As she talks, Marye is looking at some paperwork, some of the personal goals she has set for the day.

"Now look at this one," she says. "I'm a little uncomfortable with this one. This girl wants to get disability and my signature on the bottom of the page means she will get disability."

It's a common refrain. For some of the patients at the Med, "disability" is an ambition rather than a safety net. What it means is that they will be registered as disabled and therefore entitled to various forms of state and federal subsidy. The money will not be much, but it beats nothing. Marye does not approve. This is no way for a person to live her life. A person should have goals, goals for each day, each week, each year. A person should pray for God's guidance on this.

"But I don't know about this girl. Some of this shows, you know, that she is noncompliant. She doesn't always follow through with her medication. Actually I don't like that word 'compliant.' It makes it sound like I'm a judge or something. One of the things we do here is we're not telling the patients what to do. We're agreeing on a plan with them and then it is up to them to stick with it. So I prefer to say she is 'nonadherent.' Her viral load is 427. Her CD4 count is low. But she does have a history of opportunistic infection. And I suppose if you're always sick, then you can't work. But I don't know. I think maybe I'll consult on this one. She's definitely sick—but is she disabled? I don't like it when people use us to get out of paying their bills.

"You having fun?" she asks suddenly. "Because you have gotta love your job. I love my job, you know, and I always ask myself when I meet people, do they love their job?"

It's HARD TO KEEP UP with Marye's stream of words and energy, but now there's a break because it's time to see the first patient of the day. "I'm very direct," Marye has warned me. "You know, there's no point in beating around the bush. I just ask these guys, 'Are you having sex with men or women or both?' and they tell me.

"You're not squeamish, are you?"

She goes into the consulting room, where a black woman is

waiting for Marye. "She's forty," Marye says, but it would have been hard to guess. She could have been twenty-five or sixty-five. Her face has a childlike freshness, but her hands are gaunt and gnarled. Her hair is a mess and her face is a little mis-shapen, as though someone has been kneading it. For Marye this should be a routine meeting; all the patient needs is a refill of her retroviral package. But Marye doesn't really do routine, and the reason she doesn't do routine is she takes the time to find out what's going on in the patient's life. It takes a while but eventually it comes out that she has a pain in her mouth. "Open up," says Marye. "Oh, man! What have you been doing in there?"

The woman's gums on the right-hand side of her mouth are bruised and bleeding. There are fragments of tooth still in a bloodstained gap.

"I pulled it myself," says the patient with a mischievous grin.

"Well, you didn't finish the job," says Marye. "There's bits of tooth in there still. You gotta see a dentist, girl. Now you just hold tight. I'm gonna make some calls and get you sorted out."

As we go out of the room so Marye can put through the call to a dentist, I ask whether this patient is "compliant."

"Oh, no," says Marye. "I mean yes. She stays in a nursing place. She's not able to look after herself and so there is someone there making sure she takes the right thing at the right time. So in that sense she is compliant. You know, she looked pretty good today but she's not someone who is in real good control of her own life, if you know what I mean. I mean, this girl? There was a time they put her in her own apartment to see if she could make it. But one day something goes wrong in her mind and she sets fire to the whole place. She burned the whole place down. The whole apartment block, you know. And she was sitting out on the sidewalk watching the flames with a big, wide smile, wide as the Grand Canyon, and saying, 'Ain't that pretty?'"

MARYE IS A NATURAL STORYTELLER. She knows which bits to put in and—crucially—which bits to leave out. It is this skill—this gift of the gab, if you like—that enables her to be so effective at what she does. And I realize that this is a different kind of nursing. Although the essence of her job is to understand and administer various kinds of drugs, especially the range of antiretroviral remedies now available for patients who are HIV positive, it quickly becomes clear that what Marye does is talk and listen. The people she sees that day are all black, unemployed, poor. They are all HIV positive and they all have a range of "other health issues."

"What I'm meant to do is to prevent HIV becoming AIDS," says Marye. "What this means is I do everything. Pap smears, teeth, dietary advice, antibiotics. You name it. I do palliative care, symptomatic care, and preventative care. I give antiretroviral drugs. I do education."

THE SECOND PATIENT of the day is different. She's young, beautiful . . . compliant, although of course, as Marye says again, she doesn't like to say "compliant."

"Now, this little girl," she tells me in the hall, "I'm worried about her because her viral load has gone from undetectable to 9,300. And that's not good. And I'm not crazy about her blood pressure. I think maybe we have to change her medication." And she names a particular trademark antiretroviral drug that is "not working." The patient's genotype (shorthand for an assessment of the effectiveness of a drug regime) shows it's not keeping the patient's viral load down. And her blood pressure is now 140 over 98. "Way too high. Way high for a girl like this.

"So we're going to try a different combination. It's three types of pills, but Camille [the adult care pharmacist] has worked it out so she only has to take them once a day. More drugs, less often."

Over the years Marye has developed what you might call a shtick, a patter. Flirt with the boys, gossip with the girls, and throw in a bucket or two of down-home wisdom. It's never easy telling a patient that things are not going as well as hoped, but she does it with aplomb.

"So, girl, this medication we've been giving you? It's like a drink gone flat, you know what I'm saying? It ain't doing what it's meant to do anymore. It's got no fizz. So we're gonna have to change. Now, we could put you on nothing, but I don't want to do that 'cause those things you got in you are multiplying too fast for me. And I don't like that. I do not like that."

The conversation moves on to more general health matters. It is Marye's familiarity with the social milieu from which most of her patients come that enables her to get to the heart of a range of issues.

"You drinking enough water, girl?"

The woman shakes her head, but Marye won't let it slide. "Why not? Pretty girl like you has to look after her skin. You gotta keep that nice shine going. 'Cause you're looking *great*! But you ain't going to do it with no Coke or Sprite and all that. Drink water, girl. See, what I do is, I have a bottle with me all the time. I take sips all through the day."

And she keeps up this patter long enough that eventually the patient speaks, if only to shut Marye up.

"It's a family thing. My mother don't drink water. My brother don't. Ain't none of us drink water," she says.

It's the kind of revelation that can stop you in your tracks, and it speaks volumes about the social and economic roots of health and ill health. As the woman spoke, it became clear that for this woman, and for three generations of her family, water—the very stuff of life—was a kind of anathema. Water was something you used to wash dishes, or perhaps something in which you caught fish. It may even have been something you worked on, on the tows, say, that steam past Memphis every day. But it was not something you swam in and it was certainly not something you drank.

"So break the chain, sister," says Marye. "That's what you got to do. You got to break the chain. You got to look into yourself and you got to break the chain."

You don't have to listen very hard to hear the cadences of centuries of preaching in a speech like this. Marye speaks with rhythms taken straight from the sermons at the churches she has been going to since she was a child—the rhythms, and the phrases. "Break the chain, sister" clearly appeals to a real and viscerally felt sense of identity and kinship, one to which a white physician would have little access and one for which you might expect him or her to have little sympathy.

This may or may not make it effective, because the patient isn't really thinking about water and the translucent potential of her skin. What she really wants to know is whether she can claim disability, a question to which Marye has two answers. The first is professional.

"You can, but you won't get it. You have a disease, but you're not disabled. So even if I sign the form, they aren't going to approve you. They gonna look at you and say, 'What's wrong with her? She's a good-looking girl.' So you don't want to go there because if you apply and get rejected—then what're you gonna do?

"But I'll give you another answer. A pretty girl like you? No! You want a better life than that. I've never seen you not look pretty. Baby, you be fine. So you know what? Do your studies. Be yourself. Look after yourself. Don't be no person on disability."

Afterward Marye smiles at the collection of unspoken questions gathering on my face.

"Well," she says dryly, "what else can I tell her? Yes, your life is over?"

PART 2

Winter

CHAPTER 6

On Life Being Over

IT'S A COLD DAY in January—in fact it is January 7, and the temperature in Memphis is hovering a little above freezing. At the entrance plaza to the Elvis Presley Memorial Trauma Center of the Med the usual crowd is hanging around. Some are there for some fresh air; others are smoking cigarettes. And some look like they just simply don't have anywhere else to go. Inside the entrance hall, just next to the small control room where Medcom, the medical communications unit, keeps in touch with the city's air and road ambulance services, there is a little buzz. There's been a multiple shooting somewhere to the north of the city. Two ambulances are on their way. Estimated time of arrival five minutes, or, as Medcom puts it, "GSW by land in five."

As is the way of these events the details emerge slowly. First is that there are two victims. Both black. A man and a woman. "That's eight this year," says a nurse. "Seven days in and our eighth shooting. What is it with this city?"

The nurses in the trauma unit are ready. In fact the full team has gathered. Surgeons, nurses, orderlies, X-ray technician, anesthetist. ETA two minutes. Condition critical.

More details come from the radio at Medcom. Both victims have gunshot wounds to the head. Apparently it was a lovers' tiff. He loved her, but she didn't love him, so he shot her. Then he shot himself.

The ambulance sirens are audible now. A television camera crew beats them to it by perhaps twenty seconds. The camera-man has done this before. He's rolling even as he steps out of his van, and that night the shots of the two victims being stretchered into the trauma ward of the Med will be on all the news channels.

There is a flurry of activity. Behind their masks the nurses and surgeons are indistinguishable. In the corridor the hospital chaplain waits with arms folded. The ambulance crews stop for a moment to chat with the people from Medcom.

And then there is a kind of silence. Somehow, without any-one actually appearing to say it, it becomes known that both victims are teenagers. These are only kids; he is seventeen; she is eighteen, and now they're dead.

"THIS IS THE HEART of the hospital," one nurse told me. "This is why people remember us." What she meant was that other departments have their own complexities, but the trauma ward is where you either get it right or people die. Trauma is a place of drama and tension and it is a place of conflict, of raised voices and heightened emotions. It is a place of extremes, a place where a four-car pileup on the interstate can suddenly puncture the silent tedium of a "slow" afternoon.

Trauma is the part of a hospital where you expect to see blood because it is here that people are brought if they are "bent, broke or bleeding." Trauma is, in Dennis MacLannan's memorable phrase, where they take you if you're "all messed up in Memphis."

To get a sense of who it is in Memphis that is "bent, broke or bleeding," and whether this is caused by a sharp or a blunt instrument, you have only to look at the numbers. Like many public institutions, the Med is of necessity very good at documenting itself. In any year there are about 4,500 admissions to Shock Trauma. Seventy percent or more are men and 50 percent are black. One-third have no medical insurance of any kind, or—as the figures more generously put it—"thirty-three percent are 'self-pay.'"

"'Self-pay' meaning 'doesn't pay,'" I was told by many. "'Self-pay' just means they don't have insurance. The hospital will try to get the money back, but . . ."

I am struck by the consistency of the figures over the years. The average age of patients admitted to Trauma is thirty-seven. The average mortality rate is 6 percent.

It took me a while to do the math. Six percent of 4,500 means 135 people, which is to say two or three people die each week in the Elvis Presley Memorial Trauma Center. And this is despite the fact, as one nurse put it, that "for other hospitals, 'critical' is nearly dead. For us, it's manageable."

The average length of stay is 6.5 days. There are twenty-three beds available. The average occupancy is twenty-two beds. This means that there are some days—many days, in fact—when there are more patients than there are beds. It means that there are days when stretchers line the corridors and days when there are not enough surgeons, nurses or orderlies to go around.

It is the kind of place, therefore, and the kind of nursing, therefore, that appeals to a certain kind of nurse. It is the kind of place that appeals to people who work on adrenaline and who like to be tested. It appeals to the kind of people who like to see results. Many of those who work there now say they wouldn't have it any other way. Many have military backgrounds. Many are married to firemen or police officers.

There are exceptions, but Amy Delaney, RN, is not one of them.

Amy doesn't look much older than the two teenagers who died that morning. Actually, she is twenty-nine. She has straight blond hair and a friendly smile. As always with these things it is possible to do a quick calculation of where the years have gone. Amy joined the air force at eighteen. (She comes from a military family: her grandfather was a World War II veteran; her father was in the air force and her uncle in the navy.) She became an emergency medical technician, but left at twenty-two to study nursing. She graduated in December 1998, at twenty-four, and joined the trauma ward at the Med. "It was the best place to get experience. I loved it," she says. "I loved the responsibility and the trust. In here the doctors know they need us and they know we can do the stuff that needs to be done. In here we're a team, because we don't have the luxury of not being one."

"But now you're leaving?"

"Uh-huh."

"Why?"

The answer was a while in coming.

✚

It's 3:45 in the afternoon and the day shift at the trauma center is beginning the long last few hours until it's time to go home. In this department they work twelve-hour shifts, seven till seven, either "7a to 7p" or "7p to 7a." People get moved around between shifts and most will say there is not much to choose between them. A slow day shift can seem even slower than the night—and much of the "action" happens at night. Motor vehicle accidents (MVAs) and gunshot wounds often start coming in just as the shift is changing. The busy time is 7p till midnight, though in truth it is never as predictable as that. "Everything always happens all at once," a nurse told me. "It's the law of nature."

Well, perhaps. Apart from the shootings, today has been slow with not much happening. The nurses are gathered around the station in the center of the trauma ward. Amy and Ken are playing electronic Scrabble, which is what they do in those brief moments when everything suddenly goes quiet. Kerry Lyons, RN, the patient care supervisor who is "head nurse" for the day shift in Shock Trauma, is on the phone to someone in Trauma ICU. There are several different sections to the trauma center and the names reflect the presumed "progress" of a patient through the "system": Shock Trauma, Trauma Assessment, Trauma Operating Room, Trauma Intensive Care Unit, Trauma Step Down Unit and a Post Trauma Nursing Unit.

Trauma ICU is the place where critical care patients go when Trauma is full, or when the immediate work of saving their lives has been done.

Kerry Lyons

"I do this most days," Kerry says. "I chase beds." What she wants to know is whether she can have a bed for the man in bay 7. Kerry has been at the Med a good while now. She has blond hair and a curiously beady way of looking at people. She tends to purse her lips—you think in disapproval—until suddenly they break into a grin.

But not today. Today her lips are pursed for a reason.

"Uh-huh," she says. "I need one more. Uh-huh. Gunshot wound to the face. No. Self-inflicted. No, missed. Right-handed. Uh-huh, left cheek. So can I have it?"

She can and she heaves a sigh of relief. Now she just has to find somewhere for the woman in bay 5. Kerry's got only one bay free at the moment, and that's not enough because you never know who or what is going to come through the door. The doors in Trauma are kept shut, both the one to Jefferson Avenue and the one to the ward where patients are kept and cared for before they can be moved. Electronic release pads on the walls trigger the doors. Hit the pad and the door opens with a dramatic sweeping sigh. You don't have to be there long, though, to stop reacting to this sound. It may be the victim of a gunshot wound coming in—but it may also be the janitor emptying bins. Trauma is one of those places where strangers can hang around without being too obvious. In the triage unit in particular there are always strangers—police officers, relatives, undertakers— around. One more body carrying a pen and a clipboard does not look out of place. I find that the more time I spend at the Med, the more I gravitate to the trauma unit. Perhaps this is because it really is "the heart of the hospital." But perhaps it is just that in Trauma something is always happening. Other forms of medical care are slower, less dramatic. The hospital acknowledges this: "seventh January, and already eight shootings."

"There's always something," said the vice president of communications.

Now Kerry is looking to place a fifty-seven-year-old FSA, a "failed suicide attempt." At the Med they get someone like him most days, or most weeks, and it is the source of much droll humor for the nurses.

"I'll tell you what the trouble is," says Kerry. "It's that they use a .22. Those bullets just bounce around inside their heads. They want to use something bigger, like a .45. Then we wouldn't have to have this.

"And you know what? There's so much we can do these days to save people. So if you want to commit suicide, you best make sure you are good and dead. Otherwise you're gonna live—and you're gonna look terrible."

It sounds hard, but it makes people grin. Other nurses at the station offer to give lessons in suicide.

"It's really not that hard. Just point and shoot."

"Do it outside. You don't want to mess up the furniture."

Like too many others, the patient they have in today must have been a case of tortured doubt. He must have changed his mind at the last moment and, like many similar cases, he has blown a hole in his cheek instead.

"Took out some teeth, too," says Kerry, "and a bit of his jaw." Even from where I am sitting I can see the neat row of stitches along the man's face and the discolored bruising. He is heavily sedated—the pain would be unbearable—and his eyes are closed. The monitor reflecting his vital signs is calm. Everything seems in order, but, as Teddy Winney, RN, says, "If he was depressed beforehand, he is going to be *really* unhappy when he wakes up and looks in a mirror."

"These FSAs are not uncommon," says Kerry, "especially with older men."

Which—trying to shoot themselves, or failing?

"Both. You know, mostly people do this when they're alone and drunk. It's not a good time. And men do it at those times of year, you know—Thanksgiving, Christmas. They should be with a family but they're not." She shrugs. "This is the Med, you know."

"This is the Med, you know." It's a phrase I was to hear often as I spent time in the wards of the hospital. Time with nurses—but also time with doctors, cleaners, security people and administrators. It's one of those phrases that means a lot to insiders, but it takes a long time to fully appreciate its nuances and subtleties.

There are variations on it, too, which people would use when all other words failed to explain whatever phenomenon it was I was witnessing. Sharon Lucus, CRNA, who works now as a nurse anesthetist in the trauma ICU department, used it to explain the abrupt recruitment process that brought her back to the Med. She had worked previously in Shock Trauma and as a nurse on the Hospital Wing before going off to do twenty-seven months' further study to become a nurse anesthetist.

"So they gave me the job," she said, "and I asked when I should start. 'How about tomorrow?' they said." She shrugs in the telling. "The Med's the Med. They gave me one day's orientation and I started the next day."

Officer Armstrong, who works at the security desk outside Shock Trauma and who therefore witnesses the daily flow of damaged bodies that come into the Med, used the phrase in a different sense. We were standing together watching a "self-inflicted GSW" come in and I remarked on what seemed to me the extremely high levels of gun-inflicted damage in the city.

"That's the Med for you," he said, meaning that the Med gets a disproportionate share of people shooting off the sides of their faces, which is what happens when you change your mind about suicide just before you pull the trigger.

THE SHOCK TRAUMA WARD is quiet now and I take a little time to reflect on the relationship these trauma nurses have with their patients. From many snatched conversations a composite picture emerges of the trauma units and the people who work there. There is, for example, an unexpectedly high percentage of *male* nurses who work in Shock Trauma. About 20 percent of them are men, compared with 7 percent in the Med and 6 percent nationally. "But nobody ever sees that," says one male nurse. "Put one of us in scrubs and all the patient sees is a janitor or security. They don't think of us as a nurse.

"That can be helpful," he adds.

It can be helpful both because abusive patients are less likely to be abusive in the presence of Rob, who stands well over six feet, or Joel, who was a Navy SEAL and a ranking national judo competitor, and because nursing, in Shock Trauma at least, is a more or less anonymous task. The patients do not stay long enough—and are not usually in a fit state—to form relationships with the nurses. It is, in any case, something they would discourage.

All staff at the hospital carry ID tags "displayed and visible" at all times. In Shock Trauma, however, I am intrigued to notice that many have their surname "accidentally" obscured. Perhaps they have a sticker of the Stars and Stripes over it or perhaps a new lapel pin from Hospital Wing. I ask Jill, a charge nurse, why, and she tells me that they sometimes get phone calls from former patients that, "how shall I put this, we'd rather not get."

This is a very different kind of nursing from that of Marye in Adult Special Care. Here nurses ask only what they need to know. It is most emphatically not, in Marye Bernard's words, like you're "looking after family."

The "nursing model" used in the Med Trauma Center is

commonly called the case method. The idea is that it is the nurses who through the nursing process meet all the health care needs of the patient either by doing whatever needs to be done themselves or by arranging for any of the other staff (nutritionists, social workers and so on) to do so. At the end of each shift the care of an individual patient moves from the care of one nurse to another. The notes being handed on, like a baton in a race, signify the transfer. But this is a circular track. In twelve hours the baton will be handed back again.

But for the moment it belongs to Amy and Teddy.

CHAPTER 7

Cover Your Back

THE PNEUMATIC DOORS to Shock Trauma spring open, and in walk two uniformed officers with a man on a trolley bed. I don't recognize the uniforms. They're not ones I've seen before—not city cops, firemen, EMTs, hospital security, state troopers or any of the other uniformed people who come through the shock trauma unit of the Med any hour of every day.

The first thing I notice, though, is that the patient is cuffed and shackled.

"Oh, for heaven's sake, not another one," says Kerry Lyons, RN, unhappily as the two officers push the stretcher toward her. The center is the biggest, busiest level-one trauma center for miles around and deals with patients from a radius of up to 150 miles. This includes large chunks of Arkansas and Mississippi as well as Tennessee, and there are even patients coming in from Missouri. It is precisely this that causes such difficulties on the funding issue, as the state of Tennessee has to try to get the other states to pay their share for the care-and-repair of indigent people from their states.

The center opened in 1983 but it was not until 1988 that Tennessee's Licensing and Health Facilities Board designated it a level-one trauma center. This has certain consequences, in terms of both the level of care and the facility the hospital is expected to provide, and also who is going to pay for it. If the hospital cannot turn away people, then the people must pay. Patients from as far away as Kentucky and Alabama come to the trauma center.

In Trauma, service admissions are classified by "mechanism of injury." The decision to admit a patient to Trauma Service is not only on identified injury but on "the *potential* for injury due to the mechanism of injuries." Trauma means you are "bent, broke or bleeding." Injuries are also described as "blunt or penetrating." The breakdown of admissions, month on month and year on year, is remarkably consistent. About 80 percent of injuries are "blunt." Twenty percent are "penetrating." Forty percent result from motor vehicle accidents (MVAs), 12 percent from gunshot wounds. Five percent are caused by stabbing. A similar number result from pedestrians' being hit by cars. Assaults account for about 10 percent of patients in Trauma.

AND SOME ARE NOT injured at all. On this particular morning it is the uniforms that give it away to Kerry. They belong to officers of the Shelby County Jail on Poplar Avenue. By "another one" Kerry means a prisoner who she knows, just knows, will have slipped in the shower or fallen out of bed and will now be claiming to have hurt himself.

"We get maybe one a day," she says to me before calling out instructions to the officers. "You can put him in number six," she says. Kerry is the patient care coordinator, which is to say the senior nurse in Trauma today.

"Let me guess," she says to the uniformed officers with deep sarcasm. "He fell over in the shower?"

"You bet," says the officer with a grin. He, too, thinks this is little more than a charade.

"Not from his bed this time?"

"Nah."

"Y'all should put your mattresses on the floor," says Kerry. "It's not so far to fall then."

It's a routine they must have done a hundred times before. Kerry looks around to assign a nurse to the case but her team knows her well and she doesn't have to say anything.

"I'll do it," says Amy, putting down the game of electronic Scrabble she uses to fill the few slow hours in Trauma. Teddy gets up to help her. I follow them around the central nurses' station to bay 6, where the twenty-two-year-old prisoner, shackled and cuffed, is grimacing, as if in pain.

"Nobody ever got hurt falling out of bed," says Teddy once the patient is out of earshot.

"They may present with rectal failure," says another nurse, "but that has nothing to do with falling out of bed."

"Does the floor count as a blunt instrument?" asks a third.

This form of "nurse humor" covers the deep sense of frustration and irritation that this nonsense goes on. Kerry starts to "do the math." "This probably costs us five thousand dollars a visit. I'm guessing now, but if you factor in the scans, the nurses, the ambulance, it all adds up. Just the scan costs two thousand. So say five thousand and we get—what?—thirty of these a month? That's a hundred and fifty thousand dollars every month. More than one million a year." She shakes her head.

"And they say we're short of money. They all have to have everything, you see, because they all hurt everywhere. There's nothing wrong with this guy, but I guarantee he claims it all hurts."

Watching Amy and Teddy is an experience in efficiency. There's an effortless competence to their work. Teddy is medium height with strong arms and tightly cropped blond hair. He, like all the nurses, is wearing navy scrubs, the characteristic uniform of the nurses. As he checks out the patient he stands like a fighter. His weight is evenly spread on the balls of his feet; his back is straight. He is methodical and swift. He calls the patient sir and looks him in the eye as he asks questions to which Amy, perched on the next cot with a pen and clipboard in hand, writes down the answers.

They've both been in the shock trauma department at the Med for five years, and there is nothing they haven't seen. It is not surprising that Teddy and Amy are working in Trauma rather than elsewhere in the nursing field. Both came into nursing via other emergency services. Amy was an EMT (emergency medical technician) in the air force. Teddy did the same for the firefighters. Both knew they wanted more and went on to nursing school.

Amy pauses in her note taking. "A case like this," she says, "is always a major exercise in covering your back. For all of us. So I make sure the notes are pretty thorough."

"We seen this guy before?" Teddy asks.

Amy shakes her head.

"It's like *Cheers* sometimes," says Teddy. "These prisoners come in here like Norm goes into Cheers and we all sit there and say, 'Norm!' I guess they just need a break, but if this is a good time I can't imagine what they're getting away from."

Amy's notes read like this:

> 22 yo MB admitted to CCA via OAS. S/P same level fall. Pt slipped in wet shower + landed on his buttocks. C/O upper C-SP and mid T-Spine and entire L-Spine tenderness. Denies Loc. Airway patent. AAO x 3. PERRL. BS=clr. Abd soft / NT / ND. Skin W & D. MAES x 4. +pms distal. No obvious deformities noted. No bleeding noted.

One hour later, once the prisoner has been X-rayed, there is an additional note. "Discharged," it says.

Afterward I get Amy to talk me through her notes.

"So what does all this mean?" I ask.

"You want the long version or the short version?"

"Short."

"The short version is there's nothing wrong with this guy."

"And the long?"

Amy looks at the notes and reads, as though she is doing an oral examination at nursing school.

"A twenty-two-year-old black male patient was admitted to the Critical Care Area via another ambulance service (i.e., not one of ours). This is his status post a same-level fall. Patient slipped in wet shower and landed on his buttocks. He complains of upper-cervical spine (that's his neck!) and mid-thoracic spine and entire lower-spine tenderness. He denies loss of consciousness. His airways are patent. (He can breathe, right?) 'AAO times three' means he is alert and oriented, which means he knows who he is, where he is and what date it is. His pupils are round and react to light. His breathing sounds equal and clear. His abdomen is soft, nontender and nondistended. 'MAES times four' means he can move all four extremities. He has a positive pulse, motor control and senses. He has no obvious deformities and no bleeding. And no acute distress was noted.

"His vital signs were fine, too," she says. "Temperature ninety-eight, blood pressure normal, pulse eighty-eight, oxygen saturation ninety-eight."

Amy looks at me.

"There is nothing wrong with the guy. He just wants to get out of prison for a while."

"And waste your time?"

"I guess. It's not really my time when I'm here. He's wasting the taxpayers' time."

"But your back is covered?"

"Well and truly," says Amy.

Chapter 8

All This Is Temporary

At her office in the Adams Pavilion, Rhonda Nelson, RN, declines to be drawn into the question of whether or not nurses have to spend too much time covering their backs. She's been a nurse for too long to worry about that, and the view she takes is the long, long view. Rhonda is the vice president of patient services at the Med, which is to say she is the head of all the nursing staff, and whatever current problem you might raise with her, you feel that she is talking about a different timescale altogether. We're in the middle of a conversation—the sort of conversation that can be had any day of any month at the Med—about that week's funding crisis. Managing money is never easy, but Rhonda seems relatively untroubled by the stress.

"It passes," she says. "All this is just temporary. Only eternity is forever." She waves her hands around vaguely to indicate "all this." "None of this lasts," she says. Her gesture takes in her office with its furniture, nursing manuals, journals and computer. It takes in her assistant, Annie, who sits outside in an antechamber. It takes in the corridors, the trauma department across the road, the whole hospital, the city of Memphis and indeed the entire continental United States. It definitely includes me. For all I know it takes in Hawaii, the world and the universe, too. But I am unsure, because Rhonda is talking about matters spiritual rather than temporal, and my own erratic path through and then away from the Catholic Church has left me uncertain about such theological distinctions.

This is only the second time I have spoken with Rhonda, but again the discussion has quickly centered on her religion and her faith. She is curious, but perhaps not surprised, to find that I have neither. What does surprise her is that I am interested in *her* faith and *her* church. But the more I talk to her about the pressure of managing a staff of 500 nurses in a city in which the words "public hospital" and "budget crisis" are virtually synonymous, the clearer it becomes that I have to talk about her faith.

"If you're interested, then you should come to worship with me," she says.

"I would like that."

"Really? You'd do that?"

"Sure."

"Well, okay, then!" she says, lest I change my mind. And then she calls to Annie outside to see whether she can arrange directions for me to go to the Temple of Deliverance, Church of God in Christ, which is where she worships. The Temple of Deliverance is on G. E. Patterson Boulevard, a little south of the famous Beale Street in Memphis. It shouldn't be hard to find, but as I have noticed with many Americans, Rhonda insists I have a

map and good directions. Annie bustles in with them all neatly
printed out and Rhonda and I watch her bustle out again.

"I joined my new church a couple of years ago," Rhonda says
in answer to an unspoken question.

"Why?"

"My pastor now, Bishop Patterson? He is such a dynamic
teacher and preacher. He is special, if you know what I'm saying. He is really special."

"This is Pastor G. E. Patterson?"

"That's right."

"At the Temple of Deliverance on G. E. Patterson Boulevard?" I am consulting my map as I say this.

"Church of God in Christ, uh-huh," she says.

We arrange to meet at the temple on Sunday, but not before
Rhonda has had the chance to wonder again at my lack of faith.

"What you gotta think," she says, "is that if I'm wrong, then
I have nothing to lose. But if I'm right"—and here she hoots—
"boy, are you ever in trouble! You have *everything* to lose.

"And the end times are so near," she says. "Everything is
coming to pass, just like He said it would."

IN THE TIME I WAS to spend in Memphis I was to hear many
people talk about their faith and their church. People tended to
mention their congregation or their pastor early on in a conversation. It was, for many, a way of defining who they are as
much as a surname or a job title. Penne Allison, for example, is
nurse director for the trauma units.

"Her faith is very strong," Rhonda told me some months

Rhonda Nelson

later. "You know what I'm saying? Very strong." I had told
Rhonda I was going that evening to hear Penne sing in her
choir. By coincidence I had met her husband, Steven, in another
context and they had invited me to dinner. But first—would I
like to come and hear Penne sing?

I would, I had replied, and Steve met me on the steps. The
sermon at this church—the Mississippi Boulevard Christian
Church—was given by a new and dynamic youth pastor, a
woman. She wore black and she gripped the congregation in
the embrace of her powerful voice. "It was the best of times, it
was the worst of times . . ." she began, and it was a refrain she
came back to, time and time again: "It was the best of times, it
was the worst of times." And she described how at the low
point in her life, given to drink, her fiancé newly murdered, she
had found the Lord.

The congregation swayed with her words.

"She has the Lord with her everywhere she goes," Rhonda had said of Penne.

Penne, too, was swaying with the rhythms of the pastor's sermon. The church's mission was proclaimed on a large banner on the balcony railing:

We exist by God's love and the power of
the Holy Spirit to:

Mindfully move closer to God by individually
and collectively practicing spiritual disciplines;

Boldly proclaim the gospel of Jesus Christ by
witnessing locally, nationally, and globally;

Compassionately care for the spiritual,
emotional, physical, and educational needs of
God's people;

Courageously strive to alleviate injustice, racial
discrimination, and economic inequalities.

It was not incompatible, I supposed, with a career in nursing. I turned my attention back to the youth pastor telling her heartrending story of how she lost her fiancé on the eve of their marriage and how in her struggle to recover she had given herself to the Lord.

"It was a time of foolishness, it was a time of wisdom," she said.

"There's lots of us who pray," says Rhonda Nelson, referring to Penne Allison and many of her senior nurse managers. "You can't do this job unless you pray. I pray for the nurses. I pray for Bruce [the chief executive] when he goes to meet with the governor. I pray for the Med."

But her prayers are interrupted by the wailing of a siren out on Jefferson. There's been a fire in midtown, some kind of accident. It's time to go to Burn.

CHAPTER 9

Burn

THE BURN CENTER at the Med is one of the hospital's five "centers of excellence," those units in which it claims to excel. The others are the centers for trauma, high-risk obstetrics, newborns and wound care. "Burn," as everyone at the hospital calls it, is the only full-care center for a 150-mile radius around Memphis. It's housed in the same part of the hospital as the trauma unit, and you find it at the end of a series of neon-lit corridors. For most burn victims the greatest threat comes from infection, and the unit is sealed off to the outside world. It is also warmer than the rest of the hospital. If you're suffering from serious burns, you do not want to be wearing clothes. I look around and notice that most of the patients are men.

"It's kinda simple," Peggy Simpson, RN, nurse manager of the burn unit, tells me. "You know, like a man thing?" Peggy has a way of drawing out the last couple of syllables of a statement, which has the effect of turning it into a question. She and I met only recently but already we have an understanding on the question of men. Men, in Peggy's view, are simple people who would not survive long were it not for the attentions of women like herself. It's not that they are bad, exactly, or that they are stupid, necessarily, but evidence gained during her eighteen years in Burn suggests to her that men lack some of the basic cautionary instincts that come so naturally to women. One of the most common causes of burn injury, for example, is barbecues.

"Men are always in a hurry. And they have this barbecue thing, you know, that they can make a better, bigger fire than the next guy. Like it's hard, right?" She laughs. "So you can picture the scene. There's a guy and he's got a beer in his hand and a pile of wood and charcoal and what-have-you. And he's hungry. So what he does, right, is light the fire and that's okay. And he's a happy guy, you know. There's some friends around. A little music. It's Saturday night and he ain't got anything to do except drink and eat until Monday. Job's going well. Kids are doing okay in school. All's well with his world. You know? And he has a couple more pulls on his beer. But then things aren't going as fast as he would like. Maybe somebody asks him when they're gonna eat. Maybe the kids are yelling. Whatever it is, what he does is he goes to the garage and gets his . . ."

By this time I am nodding vigorously, swept along on the wave of Peggy's prose.

"Petrol," I say.

"Gasoline," she corrects me.

"He takes his gas can, and he throws—he throws!—gas all over the fire."

She looks at me with pursed lips. I am uncomfortably aware

that I have, in my time, encouraged barbecues to burn that little bit faster by throwing—throwing!—a little gas on them.

"Well! The next thing little fireman here knows is, he wakes
up in my burn unit with 80 percent burns and a 20 percent
chance of ever regaining the mobility in his hands."

I find that I have been flexing my fingers without thinking.

"My job is to take that 20/80 and make it 50/50. And that's
not easy."

No, IT'S NOT. Recovery from burn injuries takes time, pa-
tience and a lot of hard work. And it costs a lot of money. In
America more than 100,000 people require hospital treatment
for burn injuries every year. At the Med, which has the only
full-service burn unit within a radius of 150 miles, they look
after 300 admissions each year. Burn has fourteen beds, a skin
bank, an outpatient clinic, as well as facilities for surgery,
hydrotherapy, rehabilitation and research. There is a team of
eighteen nurses, of whom Peggy is, as she puts it, the "Queen
Burn Bitch," as well as physiotherapists, occupational therapists
and a team of physicians led by the medical director, Dr.
Stephen King.

Each week the team meets to review patient progress. I catch
up with Peggy as she is hurrying down the hall for the meeting.

"Burn Bitch?" I ask her. "That's a strong word."

She smiles at my squeamishness.

"It takes a special kind of person to work in Burn," she says.
"We're all type A personalities. Our relationship with the patients is different. In most places in this hospital what you have

Peggy Simpson

to do to get better is to relax, take it easy, let your body do the work. Not in Burn. In Burn if you want to get better, what you have to do is do what the nurses tell you. Because we know what's good for them."

I have heard this from other nurses, both those who work in Burn and those who don't. Not many nurses want to be a Burn nurse. Caring for fatally injured, badly disfigured and psychologically scarred patients is an emotional roller coaster. Bobby Brown, RN, who has since moved on to other wards in the Med, once believed that his mix of compassion, dark humor and searing honesty made him a natural to work in Burn. "Our unit gives patients four places to go to once they're admitted: ICU, Recovery, home . . . or heaven." After seven years on the unit he had an endless supply of shocking and horrific case studies that he's dealt with firsthand and that have left him prepared for almost any scenario. Which is just as well, because Burn tends to draw the short straw when it comes to the nursing shortage—not only do fewer nurses choose to specialize in burns, but they are more inclined to call in sick when asked to cover a shift in Burn. But Bobby would just get on with the job. "Last year we had this guy come in. He'd torched himself trying to put down a kitchen floor. He walked in here on his own, thought he'd just got minor burns—but he was one hundred percent. He just couldn't feel the pain because all his nerve endings were toasted. We had to tell him that he had only hours to live. How do you prepare for that?"

And why do you do it? What motivates Peggy? She seems to be the right person to ask because she has been "in Burn" the longest—but also because she has just announced that she is leaving.

"To do what?" I ask.

"Be a homemaker."

I let the silence ride, hoping for more. Just when I think nothing more will come, she speaks again.

"In the end there is more to life than this."

"Won't you be bored?"

"No."

"No?"

"No."

I am learning what any burn patient at the Med knows: when Peggy says no, it means NO.

CHAPTER 10

Scab Pickers

PEGGY SIMPSON WAS born in rural Arkansas just across the Mississippi River in 1967. For most of her life she lived in West Memphis. She knew from a very early age that she wanted to be a nurse and got into nursing school when she was just seventeen. "I was still a minor," she laughs. "My parents had to sign the forms." She has fair skin and brown wavy hair and looks younger—much younger—than her thirty-six years. "I still get carded," she says with mock outrage. "Still!" She is married, with two sons, whom she calls Thing 1 and Thing 2 after the characters in *The Cat in the Hat* by Dr. Seuss. It is only later that I discover that the boys were born at the Med, something too obvious for Peggy to have mentioned, perhaps. This morning she is wearing a loose trouser suit of pale green and has her hair firmly pulled back. She has bright, active eyes and an engaging smile.

"When I came here," she says, "I knew straightaway this

was where I wanted to be. This was where I was going to be happy."

This time I can let the silence ride. Peggy has pretty clear ideas on why she became a Burn nurse.

"A NURSE SHOULD BE able to work anywhere," she says. "And I could. But a nurse can only be exceptional in her niche. Burn happens to be my niche. I came here straight out of nursing school, which was unusual. They usually want you to have some more experience. But I had been through the diploma program, which offers more clinical experience while you're a student, and I guess they needed staff. Burn is always hard to recruit for. And I knew I wanted to work at the Med. As a student I did most of my practical work at Methodist. And I didn't like that."

She pauses to make sure I am keeping up.

"I didn't like that because the doctors were too important. Even at twenty I thought health care should be about a team, not about one person.

"And so we toured Burn with our class; it had been open about a year. And I knew. I just knew. Immediately. It was, like, 'Let me at those scabs.'"

Peggy laughs at the memory and at the slight discomfort of admitting there is an appeal about working with scabs.

"And so I applied and I got the job."

There must have been an unspoken question on my face. Peggy looks at me awhile and then answers it.

"I never regretted it," she says. "I'm just tired."

✚

"OH, BOY," says Bobby Brown, "have I got one sore head today. Hey, Peggy, get me a shot of something from there, will you?" Peggy Simpson turns the key on the pharmacy cupboard with unnecessary but meaningful force and gives Bobby Brown the kind of stare that stops large animals in their tracks. Bobby's sore head is a twice-weekly recurrence and is usually a consequence of a late night at Yosemite Sam's bar in Overton Square.

It's 7 A.M. on a cold day in January in the Firefighters' Regional Burn Center, better known as Burn, at the Med. Bobby looks at his drawn face in the mirror. "I always say it takes a very special kind of nurse to work in Burn, and, Bobby, you are . . . special," he whimpers theatrically.

Like Trauma, the burn unit is one of the Med's centers of excellence. Like Trauma, acute cases come to it from up to 150 miles away. Like Trauma, many of the patients coming through its doors are hours, maybe just minutes, from death. But unlike Trauma, there are no stretchers crashing through huge swing doors. Unlike Trauma, there are no stray, tearful relatives stalking the corridors in search of news. Unlike Trauma, there are no groups of nurses, medics and paramedics stopping to hold case conferences in dark offices. Instead there is just a distant and elusive hum. In Burn the overwhelming impression is of a carefully controlled, efficient and quiet environment. The calm belies the fact that this is where they deal with the most traumatic, disturbing and tragic injuries. "Burn," says Bobby cheerfully, "is as bad as it gets."

At first glance the unit appears to be an illogical weave of corridors, treatment rooms and antechambers, but it doesn't take a visitor long to learn that all routes lead back to Peggy.

IT's 7:45 AND I'm following Peggy through the labyrinthine corridors of the burn unit to her weekly meeting with the rest of the team. Nominally in charge is Dr. Stephen King,. who, like Peggy, has been in Burn for years, but really it is the two of them. They seem to complement each other perfectly, a product of both the length of their service and their contrasting personalities. Where Dr. King is genial and relaxed, Peggy is meticulous and challenging. Where Peggy is wearing a smart trouser suit, Dr. King is dressed in a T-shirt and scrubs. Both believe that health care really is delivered by a team.

We settle in for their weekly review of the patients in Burn. Gail Bridges, the clinical pharmacist for Burn, has just told me about Peggy. "When this unit loses Peggy," she said, "it will be a huge loss. She gave lots of notice, but they haven't replaced her yet. You can't just replace someone like this. Burn care is as much art as science. You can't learn it from books alone. You really have to have done it and so there's not a whole lot of places the hospital can go to find people who have done it to replace her. It's going to be hard without her."

People start coming in for the meeting. This one is held in a windowless chamber somewhere in the bowels of the hospital. The room smells of sausage and egg, of bacon and newly opened cans of Dr Pepper. The breakfast, I discover, has been provided by one of the reps for the medical companies Peggy has to deal with, and the staff members are eating hungrily.

"It's not a problem," she told me later in answer to a raised eyebrow. "All purchasing goes through central purchasing. But the reps come to me because I'm the one tells purchasing what the physicians want."

There are eleven people at this morning's meeting: Stephen King, of course, and two other doctors, one of whom is a resident. Then there are the other professionals needed to deliver full-service care to patients in Burn: an occupational therapist, a physical therapist, a psychologist, the nursing care manager and the clinical pharmacist.

Nursing for burn patients is not like other forms of nursing: the medical procedures sound the same—they may need surgery, there will be wounds to dress and medicines to administer—but the process has a quality of its own. "A lot of it is psychological," one nurse told me. "These patients try to be what they were before, but that is almost never possible. And so nursing for burn patients is very seldom about full recovery. When we do what we do—whether it's physical therapy or surgery or counseling—what we're doing is helping people understand what's happened to them." What's happened is never good, and the process of recovery takes a long time.

Today's meeting is about coordinating the efforts of the team working with each burn patient. For Peggy, the nurse manager, it is important that she makes sure each nurse knows what each of the other professionals is doing. No one is chairing the meeting, exactly, but everyone is talking to or through Peggy and Dr. King. They start with their first patient, a forty-seven-year-old man "on hospital day 46," meaning he has been in Burn for forty-six days. Forty-six days earlier he suffered 40 percent

burns to his upper body, and the care issues now relate to rehabilitation. The trouble is, the patient appears not to want to be rehabilitated. He's more interested in whether he can get certified for disability.

"No. Absolutely not," says Dr. King. "No way."

Everyone, it seems, is chipping in. The patient is unwilling to work. He lacks motivation. He just wants to get disability, even if this means he will actually be disabled. "He's the kind of guy," someone says, "who is perfectly happy to sit on the porch and drink beer all day. That's all he really wants." Which is why he won't do what the nurses tell him. "He doesn't want to get better, he wants to get certified for disability."

"Perhaps we're not being hard enough on him," says Peggy.

"He does have forty percent burns," the doctor replies.

The psychologist steps in. "We need to try and understand his viewpoint. We need to understand what things will motivate him."

"Sitting on the porch drinking beer," jokes the physical therapist. "Tell him he won't be able to lift the beer can."

But the psychologist thinks there is a better way. "His greatest fear is not having money," he says. "I think the nurses need to be very hard on this idea of disability. Tell him there is no way he is going to qualify. Tell him he can forget all that. Tell him it's work or nothing."

The difficulty, according to the physical therapist, is that this particular patient will only do things when she is watching. The moment she leaves him, he stops. "I have to neglect others for him," she says.

"What he needs," says Peggy, " is a good game of dodgeball."

Peggy explained to me earlier that one of the ways they develop, or redevelop, movement skills is by getting patients to play dodgeball in the courtyard outside Burn.

"You only like it because you're so small," says Dr. King. "Nobody can hit you."

They're all ready to move on to the next patient and the psychologist sums up.

"Your patient needs to have a clear idea of what his life will be like—if he does recover, and if he doesn't. If he doesn't put in the effort, he's not going to get certified. He's not going to get disability. And he's not going to be able to get the beer to his mouth."

A LITTLE LATER Peggy and I are talking. We're standing in one of the wide, empty corridors in Burn. I am struck again at the difference between Trauma and Burn. Here there is a sense of timelessness—in the sense that time and hard work are the healers. In Trauma, when a patient who has been shot comes in, it's seconds that count. Here it is months and years. Peggy has just told me about her decision to quit her job and I notice that she is careful to say she is quitting her job rather than nursing.

Peggy has a fierce loyalty to the unit and its nursing staff, which is rivaled only by her commitment to her family. She tried to resign two years ago, but they wouldn't let her go. She had only one demand. Now it is a precondition of her staying in her job that she leaves for home precisely at 3 P.M. "But just because I'm not here," she says, "doesn't mean they can't get me." Her beeper means that she is on twenty-four-hour standby wherever she is. "When the rubber hits the road in this department, I'm the one who's called first." Thin, with round spectacles framed by long loose curls, Peggy talks about the pressures of her job with a half-smile that says less about the kind of person able to carry it off than her hard gray and determined eyes do.

"I'm leaving for the family," she says. "I thought it would be difficult, but they make nursing so hard these days that the decision becomes easy."

"What does that mean?"

"It means that it gets harder and harder to do the things you're supposed to do. It means there is never enough. Never enough nurses, never enough money."

The beeper message is to say that a nurse has called in sick. Can Peggy find a replacement? Now? She makes arrangements, rearranges some beds. Moves some staff around. It's clear from the snippets of conversation I hear that her staff trusts her judgment completely. Peggy wouldn't be calling if she didn't need you. And so the problem is quickly resolved and she can get back to what is really on her mind.

"It takes a very special person to be a Burn nurse. I don't mean better, but a very specific type of person. All the good ones are the same. We all have the same traits, and they're not all nice."

She laughs to show she means it.

"We're very type A personalities. Everything has its place (and don't argue)! It's not enough in Burn to be assertive. You actually have to be aggressive. You know, if a doctor comes into one of our rooms without a gown, then you have to tell him to get out. You have to say, 'I don't care who you are, you don't come into my place without proper preparation.'" What she means, of course, is the constant risk of infection that all burn patients face. And there is no way she will increase that risk by letting a doctor in a hurry cut corners.

"You have to be controlling," she goes on. "You have to tell the patients that you know what is best for them. And often that means causing pain, because these are people with very serious burns, remember."

Peggy has said this before, but I have a sense now that she has been thinking about it a lot, in relation to both her patients and the life she is now going to lead. She is, for example, strict with her kids. "I am not one," she once told me, "who believes in sparing the rod." Her eleven-year-old son is the most frequent recipient of this treatment. But in matters of nursing, it is a slightly different kind of control. Because recovery hurts. If you have lost the use of your hand, to get it back you need to start moving it. But this is agonizing. Even the tiniest movement causes great pain. But without those tiny movements, your recovery will be delayed or impaired. Peggy knows this well.

"To do the things we do, to cause the pain we cause, you have to believe that you are right. It has to have a justification, and in Burn the justification, is the long-term benefit to the patient. We have to say to them that if we don't do this, then they won't recover. But if we do, they might. And that's sometimes hard."

She pauses to give the remark its due weight.

"That's sometimes very hard."

Again I have a sense that Peggy is not really talking about Burn. She's thinking of a wider world out there, of what is right and wrong in an era that sometimes appears to her to be weakening its moral boundaries.

"I just don't know," she says, apropos of nothing in particular. "People get paid millions to throw a piece of pigskin around and we have to fight to have one extra nurse on a shift." And she is lost in that thought for a while.

"The thing about Burn is, you can't choose your patients. We can't choose the patients and they can't choose the nurses. It's just like a family. Because you're going to be together for a long while. Most of the people who come into Burn aren't going anywhere for a while. That guy this morning? He's been here six weeks and he's only just beginning his recovery. And even once he's out we'll still be seeing him."

"Unless he gets his disability . . . ?"

She snorts. "Yeah, right."

For a moment I think Peggy is about to show her anger. But we're standing in the hallway outside Burn and whatever she is feeling is quickly bottled. Her face softens and seems even paler and more ghostly in the mix of sun and neon light.

"In a family you have to compromise," she says. "I tell the nurses something different, of course. I tell them, 'Listen, we are seeing people at their worst. They're in pain. They're afraid.' And the nurses know it's difficult. The patients want you to be their friend, but you're not their friend. You're their nurse.

"And it is hard for them, for patients—bless their hearts—because they have no control. They have no power. I do understand that. But it's like dealing with kids. You have to tell them, 'This is the first time you've been burned. But it is the ten thousandth time I've seen someone get burned. Who do you think knows better?'"

"And do you know better?" I ask.

"Put it this way," she says. "If it happens, I've seen it. And if they can get better, we've made it happen. This is the Med, you know."

Chapter 11

The Temple of Deliverance

It is 10:45 on a Sunday morning and I am feeling a little uncomfortable. It is not that people are staring at me exactly; more a case that I find myself staring at them and this embarrasses me. I much prefer to blend with the crowd, but on this particular morning this is not possible. For going past me in a constant stream are wave upon wave of smartly dressed men and women. The men wear dark suits and have smartly polished shoes. The women wear a peacock's array of colored dresses. They have elaborate hats and clasp delicate purses. One of them is Rhonda Nelson, RN, but I don't recognize her at first. Gone are the sober navy suits of her office and the dark briefcase of notes, policy papers and budget schedules. This Rhonda is wearing a pale cream silk suit and satin slippers, and holding a small silver purse. Her thick black tresses glisten in the spring light and she has done something to make her eyes seem bigger. She looks radiant, if a little surprised to see me.

"You made it," she says. "We should go in or we won't get a

seat. Usually I sit near the front. You'll see, there'll be a group of us in white."

Rhonda and I take our seats somewhere near the middle.

"I'll be fine," I say. "You go with your group."

But Rhonda will have none of it. "You're my guest," she says. "The Lord has sent you all the way from England to be here. I ain't gonna miss that!" She has a curious smile as she says it, aware, perhaps, that she may be on show, but that this is her home ground and to a certain extent I am on trial. For the next three hours, therefore, we sit or stand together and watch the "show." I find, to my surprise, that I am not entirely unmoved by the experience. The choir—the Voices of Bountiful Blessings—sings beautifully. Bishop G. E. Patterson, the founder-pastor of the temple, delivers a gently humorous sermon on the Holy Spirit as teacher, using as his text John 14:16 and John 14:26. He chides the followers of more extreme churches who do not take responsibility for their own lives, and he is charmingly self-deprecating. He uses Jim Jones, who led his followers to their deaths in Guyana, as the example. "Jim Jones told his people, he said, 'You don't need this book [the Bible] because you've got me.' Well, I tell you. The reason you need the Bible is *because* you got me!" During the announcements the ministry shows a brief film on gum disease and the opening prayer is simple and prophetic: "Thank you, Lord, that you have taken us from Monday through to Saturday and brought us here another day."

All things, I remind myself, are temporary. Only posterity is forever. The temple itself, a huge octagonal building, can be seen as an attempt to establish some earthly permanence, but even in its bricks and mortar there is a sense of the imperma-

nence of things. It has supplanted the smaller, more classically
designed church on the other side of the lot and it is not hard to
see the time a decade or two hence when it will have become too
small—or too big—for the needs of the bishop's ever-changing
church. I remember, however, reading Jonathan Raban's *Old
Glory* and his description of his first visit to a church in Memphis. Like me, he happened on the city by chance, and was
sucked into the eddying waters of the 1980 mayoral election.
"The churches were an extravagant proof," he wrote, "that the
black community, poor as it was, could come together to create
something just as fine as any white country club. . . . You might
live in a two-room shack with a gaping veranda, but you could
have a shareholder's stake in a real brick palace." In 1980 Otis
Higgs was the first black mayoral candidate with a shot at win-
ning. He eventually lost by a tiny margin. At the time it was seen
as a permanent defeat for black political power in the city.

But times change fast. As I listen to the music with Rhonda
swaying slightly beside me, I am conscious that only a decade
later Willie Herenton became the first black mayor of Memphis. Local journalists were in no doubt as to the significance of
the event, and the powerful politics of race that underlay his
victory: "No local event in this century has had greater impact
than the 1991 mayor's race between winner Willie Herenton, the
first African-American to be elected Memphis mayor, and the
man he beat, Dick Hackett, who may turn out to have been
the last white mayor in the city's history."

According to an article in *The Memphis Flyer* in November
1999, "This was the race that certified the passing of power in
Memphis from whites—95 percent of whom voted for then-

incumbent Hackett—and blacks—98 percent of whom voted for Herenton." "It was the best of times, it was the worst of times," said the young pastor at the church on Mississippi Boulevard where Penne Allison, Rhonda's colleague, worships. The line is from Charles Dickens's *A Tale of Two Cities,* and it seems to me in many conversations I had that there was an un-spoken—or spoken, if you asked directly—assumption that Memphis is, indeed, two cities.

"Everything in this city is about race," a journalist from *The Memphis Flyer* told me when we had lunch on a cold day in January. "Race is very important in this city," Dr. Bruce Steinhauer, chief executive of the Med, said when I interviewed him in June. It's a comment people make with certainty and in the expectation that no explanation will be needed. Perhaps the most succinct was given by Lynn Regester, RN, in October.

"It's only people with no history think this is a real nice town," she said.

As Rhonda sways with the music I take the time to reflect on the progression she represents in her own field. Only 11 percent of nurses in the United States are African-American. The percentage of African-American chief nursing officers is far smaller. But Rhonda has made it, and she has made it by skill, hard work and tenacity.

She doesn't say it, but you can sense her pride that someone like her has achieved what she has achieved.

RHONDA IS A GRANDMOTHER NOW—although you wouldn't guess it to look at her—and has been the head nurse at the Med since 1995. In one of our early meetings I noticed that she was not wearing a wedding ring.

"Divorced," I remember her saying with a tired smile. "It's okay. I thought the single life would be, you know, lonely, but I'm fine. I'm happy."

Rhonda has been a nurse for as long as she can remember. "It's been my life," she said that day. "I've done it for so long." She trained at the University of Tennessee in Knoxville. At the time Dennis MacLannan lost his arm, Rhonda would have been working in New Jersey, where she stayed for ten years. It was only in 1987 that she returned to her hometown and to the Med. And once there she progressed up the ranks: first a nurse manager, then director of nursing for Med-Surg. From there she became executive director of one of the Med's outlying clinics, and in 1995 she started in her current position as vice president of patient services.

"What's next?" I ask. "Where do you go from here?"

But there is no answer to that.

"Tell me about your job," I suggest.

"I've been through the ranks," she says. "I've done all the horrible stuff, but I've had the good times as well. Times change, but the heart of a nurse doesn't change. So when my nurses tell me, 'This is happening,' I can relate to it. I know what it's like. I've been there."

AT HER OFFICE the next day she describes her job for me.

"As chief nursing officer," she says, "what I do is to set policy. I set the standards of care and practice we expect from nurses and then I make sure that our staff are recruited and trained to deliver those standards. What I also have to do is make sure that those standards are adequately resourced. I have to make sure the money is available to pay for the people we need to deliver the care the patients expect. And the patients expect—and have a *right* to expect—the best.

"The budget is everything. Each nurse knows what it takes to care for each patient. And you don't want them going home thinking, 'I could have done better.' But the reality is that I have a budget and the budget never goes as far as you want. So I think part of my job is to shield the nurses from all that, to protect them. I want nurses I can be proud of. There's all this talk of 'magnet' hospitals, and so far—so far—no decisions have been made about whether the Med is going to pursue what they call 'magnet hospital status.' But what I feel is, and what I and Brenita [the Med's chief operating officer] have decided, is that the Med should behave as though it's a magnet-recognized hospital. Happy nurses, happy patients. That's what I want."

"And have you got it?"

Rhonda gives me a look. It is a look I am to become familiar with. It combines the qualities of an amused parent, delighted at her child's antics, with the warning that those antics had better not go too far.

"Sometimes," she says. "Sometimes we're happy."

"But it doesn't last?"

"Everything is temporary," she says. "All this."

PART 3

Spring

CHAPTER 12

Dirty Southern

TO THE EXTENT THAT Memphis is beautiful, it is beautiful in May. The blossoms have given way to the broad, green leaves of the trees along Poplar Avenue. The Mississippi River is full with the spring thaw, and the towering thunderclouds looming over Arkansas are tinged with gold and silver light. There are flowers on the magnolia trees, and the grass in Overton Park is whispering. May, not surprisingly, is the month in which the city celebrates itself. Memphis in May is, according to the organizers of its eponymous festival, "a state of mind, a long month of revelry." The month, which opens with the Beale Street Music Festival, concludes with a spectacular fireworks display over the river. There is a gentle breeze stirring the leaves on the trees that line Jefferson Avenue as I walk in to catch up with Marye Bernard in the Adult Special Care Unit.

I find her, as I so often found nurses at the Med, working on her notes. As a public organization the Med is under constant pressure to record what it does, and managers' offices overflow with reports and sheets. For the nurses the truth is that much of their work—whether at the Med or elsewhere—is a case of "covering your back," and the form this most commonly takes is "charting." You see the nurses at it everywhere. In the labor wards the forms are spread over the scales or the incubators. In the operating rooms the circulating nurse may have them on her knee or on the floor in a corner. The television image of a neat clipboard at the end of a neat bed occupied by a grateful patient may be true in some cases—in Burn, perhaps—but often it is not. And charting is one of those things that is never completed. If you have a quiet moment—well, hell, you can catch up on some of that charting. Tick this box. Check that one. There are good reasons for this, of course, and the nurses seem to take it seriously, but I find that the longer I spend in the Med, the more an image takes root in my mind. It is the picture of a nurse chewing on a pen, with a sheaf of papers in her—or his—hand.

Marye Bernard, FNP, knows the value of notes, but claims that it is as much to do with memory as with covering her back. "If I don't write it down," she says, "I never remember." And then as if to counter this she rattles off a history of one patient's medication over the past two years. We had her on this. We had her on that. Now we're going to try something else.

We start talking about money, which Marye claims is not "a big thing" for her. "Although if I'm honest, it's why I came here," she says. After working at the Shelby County Health Department, she moved to the University of Tennessee, where she worked as a clinical instructor. Her annual salary there was $51,000. "I came here, I got a three-thousand-dollar signing-on fee"—this was five years previously—"and a fourteen-thousand-dollar raise. Now I earn, what, thirty-six-plus an hour. You can work that out."

Depending on her hours, Marye earns something like $70,000 a year.

"So I came for the money and I never intended to stay. I never intended to fall in love with the job. But I know so many of the patients and I know where they live, who they are. It's like caring for my own family. I'm like a professional basketball player, you know? Like I can't believe anyone would pay me to do this."

Marye was born at the Med, back when it was still the John Gaston, and her mother was, too. In a sense this is her family. The Med, for all that it caters to the whole population, is still the hospital where most African-Americans from Memphis are born.

But for all that she eulogizes about the nursing life, Marye knows it has its limits. Her daughter, she is pleased to say, is doing her master's in computer science. "That's more my husband's area." Her husband has been a hospital administrator "forever and ever," and again I have a sense of how Marye has taken on the wisdom and posture of an age she has not yet reached.

But suddenly she is all enthusiasm again. It's time for a seminar she has organized on a new retroviral treatment. The pharmaceutical company rep is coming to talk to them and answer questions, and Marye is pleased for two—well, three—reasons.

"I know a bit about this drug," she says, "and I know the FDA thinks it will be okay. So I won't use it every time, but it will give me a choice. I like choices."

And she's pleased because most of the staff in the Adult Special Care Unit have agreed to come to the seminar, which

Marye Bernard

means that they will get their CEUs—continuing education units—and, more important, they will all be singing from the same songbook. "It's hard enough educating the patients," says Marye with perhaps a little more force than she intended.

But really she's pleased because the pharmaceutical company is paying for the lunch and Marye chanced to meet the caterer the previous day, which means the menu has changed from "dirty Southern"—"You know, when they eat spaghetti *with* their fried chicken?"—to something that, as one of the administrators put it, "has Marye written all over it": beans, okra, corn and pink lemonade. "My kinda food," she says with gusto.

Marye's next patients "tell us something about HIV in Memphis," in her words, but it is not immediately clear what. They're a couple, two men, both HIV positive. But that's not really why they've come to see Marye. They've come because they want care, care for the many health problems they display. The older one is wearing a purple tank top, black shorts and a smattering of gold. It hangs off him in all the usual places and catches the morning light when he moves. He has long nails and there is a certain camp quality to his speech. He easily matches Marye "honey" for "honey" and "baby" for "baby." He appears to be in reasonably good shape, but his companion is everything he isn't. Short. Dressed in dull workman's clothes. Stooped. He sits on a chair in the consulting room and looks at the floor. When he speaks—if he speaks—it is in a whisper and Marye has to lean in close to hear what he says.

"This one's mad at me," Marye warned me. "Because of what I decided about disability."

"You wouldn't give it to him."

"Uh-uh."

That's the third patient this morning—the third of three—for whom "disability" has been an ambition, and for whom Marye has ruled it out. "Disability" is worth—depending on the detail—maybe five or six hundred dollars a month. This is not a lot of money, but as Marye says, many of her patients are people who do not have a lot of anything. "Self-esteem, health, education. Money is way down the list of what they don't have."

This morning the older, taller man does not look mad at her. It's all "honey" this and "sugar" that and "No, he won't eat a thing," until Marye has no choice but to ask the smaller man to answer for himself.

"How you feeling, baby?" she asks.

I watch as Marye does a delicate dance through the various levels of her patient's illness. He's suffering from TB, from oral thrush. He has dandruff and tooth decay, and some kind of fungus on his face. And he's wasting away. And he's HIV positive. These are all treatable conditions—but not all at once. "There's only so much medicine a body can take," Marye says. These particular illnesses are the conditions that you associate with poverty, with nights on the street, with inadequate sanitation, with unheated rooms in dilapidated buildings and a diet high in fats and low in fiber. The Shelby County Health Department reports that 12 percent of people in Memphis and the surrounds are HIV positive. Sixty percent of these are men, and 85 percent of them are black. In Memphis HIV infection is a condition most frequently associated with being black and male and poor.

"You sore, baby?" Marye asks.

"Uh-uh."

"You have energy?"

"Uh-uh."

"You virile, sugar?"

"Uh-huh."

"He used to walk and stuff," says the taller man, "but now he don't anymore. And he coughs all the time, specially at night. He's coughing something terrible at night."

Marye gives up and asks the taller man the question she would rather have answered by the younger.

"How long?"

"Two, maybe three months."

"So, honey, we can't do everything at once. We can start fixing some things and when they're fixed we can maybe fix some more. So here's what we're going to do. First thing, I'm going to give you some shampoo, okay? I want to use it now. You give yourself a big wash. Make your hair all nice again. And then we're going to sort out some insulin for your pancreas. And you've got a temperature, so I'll give you something for that. And your thrush. You've got thrush all round your mouth— that's why he's not eating—so we'll try to fix that.

"But that's all for now, okay. You need to start eating right, exercising a little, get some strength. We need to fix that cough. And then we can start with the antiretrovirals. 'Cause until then it's just gonna be too much for your body."

It's MIDAFTERNOON sometime in May, and Marye's workday is winding down. She has seen fifteen patients—more than usual—and there's plenty of paperwork to catch up on and the next day to think about. I realize I am tired, from writing, from listening—but that she is not. She seems curiously buoyed by the day, seeming to draw strength from the tiny, imperceptible, incremental "good" she is doing.

"Good?" she says. "Maybe. I think I just like to help. These are my people. I just like to help. This is the Med, you know."

CHAPTER 13

Doing What You Can

THERE ARE NO FAILED suicide attempt victims in the trauma unit on this particular Thursday in spring. But spring is always a busy time in Trauma and today is no exception. At the nurses' station the evening shift is taking over from the day shift. Case notes are handed on. Particular problems are discussed. It is tempting to describe the scene as "chaotic," but this would be misleading. It's more the case that there is a lot of noise, a lot of movement. The critical care area is busy. The rains have brought a rash of MVAs and only two of the eleven beds are empty. There's paperwork to be completed by the day shift, details to be absorbed by the night shift. Watching the activity, I realize that one of the difficulties of working long shifts on hourly rates is there is no downtime. The patient care coordinator tonight is Yvette. There are a number of things she needs to discuss with the nurse manager, Liz. But where, and when? They have half a conversation at the station, snatch a few moments more in the corridor. In search of a moment of privacy for a more delicate conversation about another member of the staff, they take refuge in the storage closet. Meanwhile another MVA is coming in. No, two. The radio connecting Yvette to Medcom crackles to life. One is a motorcyclist. His wrist is "pretty bad." Another is a giant of a man who has rolled his eighteen-wheeler over an embankment. He's not in such bad shape.

Their arrival interrupts a conversation I have been having with David Wiener, RN, who has the distinction of having worked in the trauma departments of all the major hospitals in the city. "They're very different," he says. "I'll tell you how— but not now."

"Who decides who gets which patient?" I ask.

David dismisses the question. "You do what's necessary," he says. "You have to be pretty self-motivated to work here."

The motorcyclist arrives first. Shannon Glenn, RN, "takes" him. "I'm Shannon," she says to him. "I'm one of the faces you're going to see. But there's a lot of us, okay? Now I'm going to ask you some questions. You just answer as you can. Can you do that?"

The man nods.

"Sir, don't move your neck, please. We put the brace on because we want you to stay still. Until we've had a look at your neck, don't go moving it. Now, can you tell me these things? Who are you? Where are you? What's today's date?"

Her patient can answer all three, which makes him A&O (alert and oriented) x 3. Shannon listens carefully and asks more questions. Does it hurt? Were you wearing a helmet? She notes on her record that there is a major injury to his left wrist and some swelling on his left ankle. Before she touches him she reaches over to a dispenser of surgical gloves on the wall.

"Big, big, big. All these big boys who work in Trauma. I need small." From a box on the opposite wall she takes a pair of medium gloves from the box and as she snaps them on she continues with her questions.

"Any history of medical problems? Have you ever been in the hospital before? Are you taking any medicines?"

She is moving fast as she talks, taking his blood pressure, cutting off his jeans.

"Page X-ray, please," she says to Angela, another nurse. "We need his wrist done. We need detail."

Shannon looks at the broken wrist again. It is clearly a multiple fracture. She wrinkles her nose at it and moves on. I am struck by her easy assertiveness.

"Sir, I have more questions." The patient is moaning at the pain, but she keeps going.

"Is there anything valuable we need to lock up? Can we give your wallet to your family? Don't nod, okay? Nodding is not good. Say yes or no."

She gets his jeans off and finds another pair of shorts. And another. And another.

"Okay, you have some abrasions on your knee here. And"— here she chuckles—"fourteen pairs of pants."

Actually he was wearing four pairs, but the patient appreciates the joke and manages a weak smile, and still the questions come.

"Any back pain? Do you smoke?"

"Only marijuana," says the patient, to my surprise but not, evidently, to Shannon's.

"You have to be very assertive," I say to Shannon, taking advantage of a brief pause while she waits for someone to help "roll" the patient off the ambulance board and onto a hospital bed. "I'm impressed by how easily you take charge."

"Yeah," she replies. "There's no choice, really. If you don't get them to do things your way, they're only going to hurt themselves." She indicates his neck. "You don't want them to go shaking their heads until you know what the damage is." Shannon is perhaps thirty. She has fair Irish skin and today her cascading brown hair is held firmly in check. Like everyone else she is wearing the anonymous blue scrubs that contribute to the patients' feeling that she is just "one of the faces you'll see around here."

The X-ray technician comes in with the machinery and takes shots of the patient's wrist.

"You got a wife?" Shannon asks the patient. Despite the brace, he nods again. "You have? I think your easy riding days may be over. That's some serious bone soup you got there."

Twelve hours later I was to meet that bone soup again—in the operating room.

IT TOOK A LITTLE longer to understand why Amy was leaving.

I am about to ask Amy Delaney why, when she is summoned for a meeting with the nurse supervisor. A momentary wave of alarm seems to wash over her and I assume she is trying to remember any mistakes that might require a reprimand. In practice it turns out only that she has been more than twenty minutes late three times in a week and she is due for a formal reprimand and warning. Her nurse supervisor is Liz.

"I have a lot of time for her," says Amy. "Not right now, but generally." She laughs but others agree. The nurses have a finely tuned appreciation of who in the hospital's administration is "on their side" and who is not. The CEO, Dr. Steinhauer, for example, has tremendous respect from the nurses because when he is in Trauma and all hell is breaking loose, he is not afraid—or too proud—to do whatever needs to be done. He has been known to push trolleys in his time as CEO, and when he visits the wards he makes sure he is carrying a stethoscope.

Her uncomfortable moment with Liz passes and eventually Amy and I get to the question of why.

Perhaps not surprisingly she starts talking about money, but the more time I spend with her the less I think money is what matters to her.

"The thing is," she says, "I'm not leaving nursing. I'm going back to school. And there are layers to this. I've been accepted to study to become a nurse anesthetist and that's what I'm going to do. When I finish I'll earn twice what I earn now."

Which is?

"Last year I did fifty-three thousand, gross." Amy takes me through the calculations. To a basic rate of $21.50 per hour she adds various differentials: $3.00 for weekends; $2.50 for weekdays after 3 P.M.; $3.50 for weekdays after 11 P.M. Her husband is a fireman. I am surprised to learn later that as a nurse Amy is already earning more than a fireman or a police officer on basic pay. Because they're not keeping up with other professions. A July 2002 report by the Health Resources and Services Administration reported that one key reason for the diminishing supply of nurses was wages. "In 1983 the average elementary school teacher earned about $4,400 more than the average RN; by 2000 this had grown to the point where elementary school teachers earned about $13,600 more."

"It's really hard to work out how much you're going to get at the end of the month. But a nurse anesthetist will start at twice that," she says, and gives me the name of a Web site where I can look at what people are earning. "And that's just to start." To pay for the twenty-seven months it will take her to train as a CRNA, Amy will take out the $18,000 student loans available to her annually, and other than that she will live on her savings and on her husband's salary.

"And once you've done all that, then you can have kids?"

"Maybe." She smiles. "When I've earned a bit and paid off my loans. I still have loans from the last time," she says.

It's a calculation the nurses make a lot. Sharon Lucus, a CRNA in the Trauma ICU, has trodden the path down which Amy is headed. Sharon is now thirty-eight. She has a twelve-year-old daughter (born before she became a flight nurse at Hospital Wing, the helicopter unit that serves the Med and three other hospitals in Memphis) and a three-month-old son. Sharon is something of a mentor to Amy, and her career follows an uncannily similar trajectory. Like Amy, she comes from a military family. Like Amy, she values her time in the trauma wards. "It gives you the experience," she says. "It gives you autonomy. People trust you there." And, of course, it gives you the kind of clinical experience you need to get into anesthesia school. It also shows the dean of that school that you're the kind of person who will make it, the kind of person who doesn't give up easily.

"It was the hardest thing I ever did," Sharon Lucus said the day before. "I quit several times, and each time the dean brought me back in. Now it's the best thing I ever did."

Where Amy differs from Sharon is that Sharon is now glad to be back at the Med. "I could be making twenty thousand more working at Methodist," she says, "but the amount of autonomy I have here makes it worth it."

Perhaps the figures are exaggerated. Perhaps the differential would be $10,000 a year, but even so, it strikes me as a heavy price to pay for something as intangible and ephemeral as "autonomy." It seems to me that a management that can sell this to its staff, without compromising quality of care, is either very good or very lucky, or both. "Our wages have kept pace," Rhonda Nelson told me when I asked her. "These nurses are paid okay."

Sharon Glenn, meanwhile, tells me the story of the sixteen-year-old kid from Germantown who was brought into the Med the previous week. "And his parents were, like, 'This is better than on TV!' but when they went out the front entrance they were still afraid of being mugged."

GERMANTOWN IS the smart part of Memphis, the kind of area where row upon row of $3 million homes are not uncommon, the kind of place you go to live when you've made it.

It is also where Amy hopes to work once she has qualified as a CRNA.

"You won't come back to the Med?" I ask.

"No. Give me regular hours, a clean hospital—you know, patients who don't throw up on you. That and double the pay. That's where I'm headed."

She takes a sip of her raspberry tea and stirs it with a straw.

"The most disappointing thing about this job is that you study so hard, you *work* so hard, and people don't appreciate it. The patients don't appreciate it. The management don't appreciate it. Nurses are always in the middle and it's not a good place to be. That's why I'm getting out.

"Where I work, in a critical care area, often you get the best nurses. The ones who really know what to do. But that's not what the patient remembers. The patient remembers the pain and the mess. And if he's grateful to nurses at all, he's grateful to the ones he sees when he starts to get better. And that's not us. We're exposed all the time—to HIV, to hepatitis C, to violence. We're exposed every day and eventually it's not worth it. The good days are just too far apart.

"You remember that guy," she says, "yesterday. The one who 'shot himself' and had a security alert on him?"

I do. It wasn't clear to me (or, I thought, to others) exactly who had done the shooting, and the constant presence of the police suggested they had their doubts, too.

"I see that too much. People lying in our beds wondering whether their friends are going to shoot them."

I remember an incident the day before when a pregnant survivor of a motor vehicle accident came in. I remember the blood dripping onto the floor while the resident catheterized the traumatized woman, who had no way of knowing yet whether her baby had survived. I remember how the team of nurses, including Amy (but anonymous in their OR masks), worked to make her as comfortable as possible. And I remember thinking I wouldn't want to do that, day after day.

"It takes a while to figure it out, but eventually you feel it's all for nothing, and that's why I'm getting out."

Not yet she isn't. Amy has another couple of months to go before she has the luxury of being a student again.

It's 6:15 p.m. in the trauma ward and everyone seems a little on edge. People are watching the clock. Quiet days can be the worst. They drag on and especially in the early heat of spring patients' tempers fray more easily and the nurses are a little on edge.

One patient, a tall, strong man with a gunshot wound to his right temple—the bullet grazed him—and some upper-body bruising, has a hangover. He's coming out of a long drunk and he doesn't feel too good about the world. He's starting to curse. The nursing assistant has brought him back from the CT scan unit for the second time, where he is refusing to lie still. CT uses a computer and a rotating X-ray device to create detailed, cross-sectional images, or slices, of organs and body parts.

A CT machine resembles a large, square upright doughnut

Kerry Lyons

and is commonly used in Trauma because it "reaches the parts X-ray cannot see." A flat "patient couch" is situated in the circular opening, which is about twenty-four to twenty-eight inches in diameter. The patient lies on the couch, which can be moved up, down, forward and backward to position the patient for imaging. The CT scanner itself is a circular, rotating frame with an X-ray tube mounted on one side and a banana-shaped detector mounted on the other. A fan-shaped beam of X-rays is created as the rotating frame spins the X-ray tube and detector around the patient. For each complete rotation, one cross-sectional slice of the body is "acquired."

For a CT scan it is customary to tape the patient's head to the trolley to make sure he doesn't move. But this man is having none of it—and he's hard to persuade.

Kerry, whose husband is a police officer, is unmoved.

"Sir, you have no call to speak to us like that."

The patient is cursing her crudely now. His swearing is ugly, sexual, personal.

"Get security," says Kerry quietly. "Now."

She turns to address the man again.

"Sir, you are free to go, but if you do, it will be against medical advice. You can refuse to be treated, but then you must go. But if you stay, then you are not going to tell us how to take care of you."

"I couldn't breathe," says the patient, and he holds his hand against his throat to show how he was choking. "They make me choke on my spit." He swears at Kerry again, a verbal version of the violence that so often comes through the doors of the shock trauma wards.

"Sir, you have a choice," says Kerry, ignoring the insults. The security people have come but at a signal from Kerry they hold back. She has it in hand. A couple of other nurses gather around, male nurses. "I'll take him back," says Rob.

"Okay. I'll call ahead. See if they can do it without taping."

Amy meanwhile is on the phone. "Yes, sir," she says, "when I transfer you, ask for 'unknown trauma 523.' That's what it will say on the files."

And beside her Teddy is giving discharge instructions to a patient's relatives. "He'll be staying with you?" he asks.

"Uh-huh," says the woman. "With me and my son and also with another person."

She sees the slight worry on Teddy's face.

"Let me put it like this," she says, "We're a very dysfunctional family."

Teddy smiles. "You are not alone," he says.

Rob comes back with the abusive patient. "Did it," he says. "He cooperated."

Kerry sighs. "I hate days like this," she says. "I'd much rather have something to get stuck into."

"Definitely," says Amy, picking up the electronic Scrabble set. "But not now. Now we need nothing to happen for"—she glances at the clock—"thirty-five minutes because in thirty-five minutes I am *outta* here." But at this moment the radio on Kerry's hip crackles into life. There's been an MVA. Three injured. The ambulances are five minutes away.

"Stand by," says Kerry, but Amy is already tying on her mask.

"I'll still be here in ten years' time," says Kerry in the quiet of those five minutes. "This is what I'm good at."

CHAPTER 14

A Child Is Born

IT WOULD BE NICE to think that Dr. Sheldon Korones will be at the Med in ten years' time. He runs the Newborn Center, part of the birthing and delivery unit at the Med—and he's been doing it for the past thirty-five years. It takes up an entire floor of the Rout Center (named after a former mayor of the city), which includes the maternity wards and a high-risk obstetrics unit. The Newborn Center has about seventy beds and provides intensive postpartum care for newborn infants. It is one of the oldest and largest newborn intensive care units in the United States. It is one of only fourteen member institutions of the National Research Network, which is supported by the National Institutes of Health Child Development Program. Perhaps 30 percent of the 4,500 babies born at the Med each year need to be looked after in the Newborn Center.

Shelby County and the city of Memphis exceed the national average in virtually every measure of health regarding new-

born babies. It has twice as many children born with low or
very low birth weights per 1,000 patients. Nationally about
11.4 percent of births are premature. In Memphis the figure is
15.6 percent. Nationally there are 7.2 deaths per 1,000 live
births. In Memphis the figure is 13.2. And so on. By all these
measures the Newborn Center at the Med is coping with a dis-
proportionately unhealthy population. The same is true of
other departments. Memphis has nearly three times the national homicide rate (measured as per 100,000 population): 20.2
compared with 7.2 nationally.

The figures break down further, and more worryingly, by
race. The infant mortality rate among white children is 5.8 per
100,000 population, compared with 6.0 nationally. The infant
mortality rate for black children is 18.7.

"And that's what we're dealing with," says Dr. Korones.

He pauses to reflect a moment before starting a new thought.
"I suppose we must have cared for something like forty-five
thousand newborns," he says with a smile. "Something like
that, here at this center. At the peak in this hospital we had
eight thousand deliveries a year, but now we're delivering four
or five thousand. And of those, maybe a quarter or just under
come to us, here at the Newborn Center."

"That's a lot of babies," I say.

"I've been here a long time."

"But forty-five thousand?"

"Well," he says, "when you think about it, it makes sense."

And in a mathematical way, I suppose it does. Since Dr.
Korones set up the Newborn Center in 1968, the Med has
delivered well over 100,000 babies. But in another sense the

number seems too big for one doctor. The 45,000 babies Dr. Korones refers to are not the total number born at the Med. It's the number of kids he has had in his personal care in the Newborn Center, which is where you go if you need special care once you are born. I try—and fail—to imagine a life spent supervising the postpartum care of 45,000 children. I try—and fail—to imagine whether the elation of each birth outweighs the occasional death. The mortality rate in the sixty-bed newborn intensive care unit that Dr. Korones has managed for thirty-five years hovers around 2 percent.

I'm meant to be spending time with the nurses in the Newborn Center, but I know that it is wise to catch up with Dr. Korones first. He has, as he puts it, been there a long time. Now seventy-nine years old, Dr. Korones qualified in 1947 and has been practicing medicine ever since. I ask him what keeps him going as a doctor, nearly fifty years after he first started practicing.

"What else could I do? What else would I do? I could die, I suppose, but where's the fun of that?" Jokes aside, Dr. Korones has an agenda. "The fundamental mistake," he says, "was to make health care a product, something you sell. And a good part of my motivation is to fight that. Medical care is not a product. It is not something you should buy and sell. It is a right, not a privilege. If you want me to be grand about it, I'd put it like this: it is a moral and constitutional right, part of our guaranteed right to life, liberty and the pursuit of happiness. You can't be happy if you're sick.

"When someone is sick," he says, "I am compelled to take care of him. I don't ask whether they can pay. I do what I can."

Dr. Korones's beliefs were influenced by his roots in the Jewish Diaspora. His grandfather, a refugee from Cossack raids on his native village in the lowlands of southern Belarus, arrived at Ellis Island in New York City on the day that President McKinley was shot. "That made it hard to forget," Korones says, smiling. "Six September, 1901. They talked about it all the time."

He was born in the city in 1924 and largely raised by his grandparents.

"They would tell me stories," he says, "of the old days. And when people ask me why I became a doctor and when they ask me why I make such a noise about medical care being a right, then I tell them about my grandfather's toes."

I look at him. "Toes?"

"He was missing five toes. He would take off his shoes and show me his toes and tell how he had to escape. He lost them to frostbite one winter while he was hiding from the Cossacks. And the thing was, that shouldn't have happened. It was wrong. I grew up with a very strong sense of what was right and what was wrong."

Korones is not a big man, but he stands tall and dresses smartly. He looks in extremely good health and speaks with a clipped New York accent. He regrets that he doesn't speak Russian but is proud that his son, also a doctor, has learned it. On the wall is a plaque commemorating the recent visit the two of them made to Mogilev, the town from which his grandfather fled.

"So for a while I was in private practice," he says. "Pediatrics.

But I realized that all I was doing was making money. And what good was that to me? How much can one man spend? Now, what I do is like a religion with me. We must take care of people when they are sick. I think there is something wrong with us if we don't see that. This business of making health care a product, something you sell? For me this is a historic crime. Here at the Med we are catering to a public that will never be able to pay. Fine. We still cater to them—and the money will have to come from somewhere else."

Dr. Korones is watching to make sure I am keeping up. I can tell from the rhythms and the practiced phrasing that this is a speech he has made before. Indeed, I have heard some of it before. He gave me the same speech back in January, on my second or third day at the Med. And so I nod. I am keeping up.

"So I came to work here. This hospital is where it was happening. And I came here knowing that it would be different. If I work in a private ward, I'm the doctor. I'm it, you know? But that isn't the way here. Here we are a team. And I knew here that nurses would be the key. A hospital like this, catering to a population like the one we serve? These places can only be as good as their nurses. It's been my philosophy all the way through. Give me mediocre doctors and superb nurses any day instead of vice versa. We're a team here and in a team everyone matters. Of course, the hierarchy must stand, but there must also be a free exchange of ideas. Especially because this is a teaching hospital and often in a teaching hospital the doctors-in-training know less than the nurses in some areas."

He takes a breath, while I continue to scribble.

"Let me put it another way," he says. "This is a black man's hospital. I've stayed because I can make sure they get the best treatment, the same as any hospital in the city. I couldn't do that anywhere else. I can only do it here."

He pauses.

"So I knew some people, and we raised some money and I started the Newborn Center here at the Med in 1968."

Dr. Korones pauses to see that I have understood the significance of the date. "We aren't poster-carrying people, you know. That was never my style. My father—he was a Republican—big R, small r, whatever. I didn't grow up marching or protesting or any of that. But I did understand something about what it is to be human. So then in 1968 I was in private practice, doing my thing. But back then we had all these other things going on. [Robert F.] Kennedy. [Martin Luther] King. And people had to respond to what was happening around them. My response was to start this place. I was in a position to do something and I did it."

Chapter 15

A Process of Weaning

Kerry Lyons, the patient care supervisor in the trauma unit, speaks about her work at the Med in the same way. It puts her in a position where she is able to do something—and she does it. It's this thought that underlies her assertion that this is where she belongs, and this is where she will be in the years to come. Despite his protestations, it seems the same might be true for Bobby in Burn. Living on his own in central Memphis, in the middle of the city's bohemian district, he talks about his nursing career as though it's a stopgap. But now he's been at the Med too long and his vague noises about moving on are unconvincing. This is good for the unit. He and Peggy have clearly formed a partnership that works. Together they provide enough mental toughness, clinical experience and gallows humor to sustain the team of nurses, physiotherapists and psychologists who, even by the Med's exacting standards, are severely stretched.

"You know why we're stretched?" he says. "I'll tell you

why. Too many people die in Burn. It gets some nurses down. You know?"

Because inasmuch as there is a stream of new nurses coming into the profession, the majority are attracted to the high-profile ER and trauma units. These are the glamour end of hospital medicine. At the Med it is no different, with Neonatal and ICU also heavily favored. By comparison, Burn is an afterthought.

TODAY, HOWEVER, there's the promise of, so to speak, new blood in the unit. Sheila, one of the Med's nurse orientees, has made a special request to spend time in Burn, as she's seriously considering making it her new specialty. She's an RN new to Memphis with excellent qualifications and six years of hospital experience. Why would she want to come to Burn? "Maybe she heard about the wet T-shirt competitions in the hydro room," Bobby speculates. The hydro room is where all burn admissions go first, to receive a heavy dousing of water while wound cleaning and assessments are made. Working in Burn requires a special kind of humor.

A new nurse would be very welcome right now but Peggy retains the right to be fussy in the extreme about who joins her team. "Listen," she says, "some of my nurses will spend half their lifetimes in this unit. Doctors come and go and I tell all the new ones that they are just guests here—this is our home. It's nurses who make this unit what it is and you have to be a special kind of person to fit in." One doctor who receives a warmer welcome than most from Peggy is Dr. Stephen King, MD, the unit's medical director. In his late forties, square-jawed, light brown skin, distinguished graying hair, he has a noticeable but

not impolite amount of stubble—regulation *ER* casting. He
and Peggy have a quick discussion about a patient who is almost ready to transfer from the burn ICU to Step Down, the
first crucial stage in her rehabilitation. Bobby explains that
Burn is like a hospital within a hospital, including surgical, intensive care and rehab facilities. "Yep, there's only four places to
go when you come to Burn: ICU, Step Down, or home."

And the fourth?

"Heaven."

"OKAY, SO IN HERE we got a female patient. She's got a BI [burn
index] of eighty-one, " Bobby says. It's hard for Sheila to see the
patient at first. Beneath a mountain of swaddling the shadow of a
nose is visible, possibly also a bunch of wispy gray hair. She is in a

Peggy Simpson

dark, sealed-off room, divided from the ICU's general floor by a large sliding glass door. Infection is the greatest enemy for a burn patient, and it looks like she is well protected. But, says Bobby, she won't live much longer. "No one could, not when they look like that." The BI that Bobby refers to is a calculation that takes in the age of a patient and the percentage of the body affected by first- and second-degree burns, to yield a mortality rate. "I don't think she'll see out the next two weeks," Bobby concludes.

"But that doesn't mean we won't give her maximum care," Peggy jumps in. "We can't save her life but we'll manage her pain until the end."

"Next up is a forty-three-year-old man, and he's been in ICU for three days," says Bobby. He rolls his eyes. "Oh, man, this was re-e-al nasty. His girlfriend boiled up a big vat of sugar water and threw it over his lower abdomen and groin area." Sheila looks visibly shocked. "By the time he got in here it had caramelized. It was like cracking a crème brûlée." The patient will survive but his life, as with so many of the patients who come through Burn, will never be the same again. It's one of the hardest lessons new nurses like Sheila have to learn—there's very seldom such a thing as a full recovery in Burn.

"And in here we've got a little girl. She's got upper-body burns from a trailer fire," Peggy says. Beyond the glass Sheila can see two figures. One is the girl, small and motionless in her bed. The second is a woman, presumably her mother, sitting in the darkest corner of the room. She is as still as her daughter.

"Sheila," Peggy says, "if you join this unit and you stay with this unit, then you will get to know her very well." Her point is that even if the girl makes a good recovery, years of aftercare await her. Providing her family stays in Memphis, all of it will happen here at the burn unit. As she gets older her skin will no longer be able to grow with her, leaving her body locked inside. She'll need regular trips to the unit for surgery to release the pockets and sections of skin. "Yup," says Bobby, "once a Burn patient, always a Burn patient.

"And this is where it all kicks off." Bobby is showing Sheila around the hydro room. The central features are a vast water tank and three metal beds, each surrounded by a trough and, overhead, large shower jet heads. Before Bobby gets a chance to show Sheila any more of the room, there's activity outside. Peggy steps in quickly. She says something to Bobby about a "big one." It turns out she is referring to a fire in an industrial plant in western Tennessee. Three ambulances are already on their way. More nurses pour into the room. There is a low buzz as cabinets are opened, lotions prepared, water flows tested. "Sheila, you better put your blues on," Bobby says. "You're about to get an A-plus education in nursing for burns."

NONE OF THIS COMES CHEAP, and from time to time the Med's management analyzes the costs. It doesn't take long to see why the Med is in perpetual financial crisis. Take, for example, the second half of 2002. In that time 249 patients were admitted to Burn. They stayed for an average of one and a half days per 1 percent of burn (the palm of your hand is roughly the equivalent of 1 percent) and so a patient with 50 percent burns stayed, on average, seventy-five days. The total charges for those patients came to $9,565,508. But the total recouped was only $1,974,836. Burn does, and almost always has, operated at a huge loss.

It's not hard to see why. Nearly 40 percent of those 249 patients were "self-pay," which is to say uninsured . . . which is to say "no-pay." Of the $3,657,654 billed to the eighty-six self-pay patients, only $2,723 was ever received. Out-of-state Medicaid—any other than Tenncare—was not much better. For these patients there was only a 5 percent collection rate on billings. This is clearly not a basis on which to run a business. Equally evident, there is a need for the service, but even with the insurance payments received, the collection rate for the whole unit is little more than 20 percent.

At the Med it happens, and Peggy has seen it. I join her just as she is about to go home. I'm interested in pursuing some of the metaphors she has been using, of how caring for patients with long-term needs is different from caring for patients whose needs are more immediate. In the shock trauma wards, nurses have told me that the reason they want to work there is they like results. For Joel, a thirty-two-year-old former Navy SEAL, the appeal is exactly that. "They need to be fixed and we fix 'em. And then they're gone. We don't have to have relationships with these people."

Peggy does have a relationship with "these people" and it is a delicate one. As we are leaving she shows me the partially closed door to one of the rooms in Burn. Inside is the recalcitrant patient who lacks motivation and who wants—so it is said—nothing more than to sit on the porch all day and drink beer.

"Why is it closed?" I ask.

The answer is that it is part of a process of "weaning," as Peggy calls it, the patient off his dependency on the nurses.

"Being burnt messes you up pretty badly," says Peggy. "And you want to be taken care of. But sooner or later they're gonna have to take care of themselves. For him it's sooner."

PEGGY LIVES in a pretty subdivision on Mud Island in the Mississippi. There have been heavy rains recently and the river level is rising. In the 150 years since the U.S. Army Corps of Engineers took control of the river, they have developed an extremely sophisticated method of monitoring its flow and predicting flood dangers. This doesn't always work. As an engineer at the Waterways Experiment Station in Vicksburg, Mississippi, once told me, "Mother Nature is not predictable." But it has given rise to a common terminology. At Memphis the main gauge is 1,800 feet downstream of the Hanrahan Bridge. The highest reading on record was during the great floods of 1937, when the river at this point crested at 48.7 feet. The lowest ever was minus 10.7 feet during the drought of 1988. That's a range of nearly 60 feet, which is a lot. As Peggy and I drive over the bridge onto Mud Island, the area of Memphis most vulnerable to flooding, the river is at 29 feet and rising, which is not so unusual for May. "They say it will crest at thirty-four feet," Peggy says, pointing to a front-page photo in that morning's newspaper. It shows some kids playing beside the river on Mud Island, and with a hint of pride she points out her son. "Doesn't he look cute in those boots," she says. This is a flood level, but not a dangerous one. At 34 feet on the gauge, waters will start to inundate the floodplains of Arkansas.

"But we're used to this," says Peggy. "We don't start to get worried for a good few feet yet."

We turn north to the recently developed tract of smart houses and impeccable sidewalks on Mud Island. Not a blade of grass is out of place. Peggy and her husband moved to this house three years ago. Prior to that they lived in West Memphis. Now the boys attend a nearby Montessori school and Peggy has only a ten-minute commute to the hospital. But you wouldn't know it from the place. This part of Mud Island feels like it is a million miles from the dirt and grime, from the pain and suffering of the Med. Here each house looks perfect, its white clapboard and pastel trim glowing in the late-afternoon light. The residents smile and wave to one another and the dogs never bark.

Or so it seems.

"I apologize for the mess," Peggy says, to my confusion. She said the same in her office, but there I understood because at the Med she works in a riot of paper, medical samples, discarded scrubs and the plethora of magazines, manuals, circulars, notices and forms that are the bread and butter of any nurse manager's life. But here?

While her sons are doing their music lessons—a necessary chore before heading out for a Little League doubleheader—Peggy and I talk some more. We are upstairs in her house in a little den overlooking the river. Below us what is normally field is now covered in water.

"It's one of the reasons we bought the place," she says. "Not now, of course, not when it's like this. But when the water is down, all that out there"—she points to the oaks, the mimosa and the cottonwoods rustling in a gentle breeze—"all that is just boy heaven."

And I think for the moment I glimpse the real Nurse Peggy.

"I'm leaving for my family," she says. "I'm leaving because the boys need me. Everything starts with the family, and if we don't get control of our kids things start to deteriorate." Peggy is trying to create a piece of boy heaven, and if that means withdrawing from what seems like her second home, the Med, then so be it.

"So I'll be a full-time mom, for the summer at least. Financially, do I need to work? I don't know. My husband has a good job." (He manages an Internet team for a Fortune 500 company.) "And he thinks I will go stir-crazy. But I'm not sure. I think it will be okay."

I think it will probably be okay, too. Peggy is on the way up, and it is not about money. I have a sense that nursing, and all the rules and controls she made to go with it, have hemmed her in. For sixteen years she has remained true to that original impulse that drove her into Burn. But now things have changed, and what has changed most is Peggy. She is no longer the driven nurse, and no longer the young girl with memories of a poor childhood in rural Arkansas. She has become someone altogether more confident. And I have a sense that she will blossom with her time and her newfound freedom. As she shows me around the house, and as her face lights up with delight at the artifacts made by her son and bought—"in competitive auction!"—at the school fete, I have a sense that for the first time she feels free.

She once told me that "you only work at the Med if you want to," but it seems to me, from listening to Peggy, that for many, you only last as a nurse if you need to.

But Peggy no longer needs to.

Chapter 16

Talking Budgets

Rhonda Nelson has stayed the distance and made it to the top of her field. In her office the Med's most senior nurse reminds me that she has come up the hard way. There are precious few nursing jobs she hasn't held at one time or another, both at the Med and elsewhere.

"And I know that it's a hard job," she says. "I know that it's thankless. I know that. What you have to understand about the Med is that the doctors and nurses here are very talented. For nurses in America this is as bad as it gets. They see the worst. They see the gunshots and the accidents. They see all the babies born before term. They see all kinds of stuff. To work here you have to have a passion. It's like a ministry—you know what I'm saying? The nurses here have a desire. They *want* to be here, and they are trained for the worst, which is the best sort of training for a nurse. That's very clear. The Med is *the* place to be in terms of getting your skills. If you can work at the Med, you can work anywhere."

This is another refrain that I am to hear often. Many nurses tell me they can but wouldn't work anywhere else. The pay at the Med is commensurate—or not much less—than at other hospitals, but what they get at the Med cannot be underestimated. For here, under Rhonda's regime, they get the intangible things that they think are harder to come by in other hospitals: respect and autonomy. Respect from their peers and the physicians; autonomy in their work. These are things you cannot easily put a price on. There is a silence and I take the time to look around the room. It doesn't look like the office of someone who has been there for eight years. There is a sense of transience, the feel of a hotel room. It has the look of a place Rhonda could vacate in minutes.

"Well, you picked a fine time to visit," she says with a laugh. "They're about to close us down."

This is a reference to the current financial crisis. I discount it slightly. The Med was in a financial crisis when I visited a few months before and it was in a financial crisis eighteen months previously. I doubt there has ever been a time when the Med was not in a financial crisis of one sort or another.

"But this one is worse," she says. "This one is really bad."

OVER THE COURSE OF several visits to the hospital I was to hear many variations on this theme. Sometimes people would take the view that "they'll never close us down" because this would only send the problem elsewhere. Others take a gloomier view. "The state has always hated us," they say, partly because the hospital's position in Memphis means that it caters to citizens from Mississippi, Arkansas and even Missouri, as well as local residents in Memphis and Shelby County. But it is the residents of Shelby County who pay the most. In his article in *The Commercial Appeal,* Lewis Donelson, chairman of the board at the Med, has made the case that the Med is, in fact, a net contributor to state funds, but that this is never acknowledged. Because of the public access care it provides, the state of Tennessee can claim federal matching funds from Washington. In the current year, Donelson calculates, these amounted to nearly $50 million, but rather than pass these funds to the Med, the state prefers to spread them among all nine public access hospitals.

Nowadays Memphis is the eighteenth-largest city in America, a place of history and beauty, but also a place of poverty and decay. As the city's leading public hospital, the Med caters to a diverse population, and competes in that uneasy space between private and public provision. Public officials readily acknowledge the need for the services the Med provides—it is the largest of nine such hospitals in Tennessee—but they are far less ready to write the checks that make its existence possible.

The Med's "safety net" status enshrines its commitment to provide for people with limited or no access to health care, and nowhere else in the city's medical establishment are the resources so scarce, the patients so sick and the staff so stretched. Much of this derives from its complex relationship with the state of Tennessee. The hospital has an annual operating budget of about $250 million. The day I met Rhonda and agreed to go to church with her was forty days short of the end of the Med's fiscal year, and the hospital was predicting a $13 million shortfall in its budget. This is the scale of deficit that threatens not only patient care but the whole hospital, because if it is not resolved it will happen again in the coming year and the year after that. If there is a year after that. The evidence is all too easy to read in the minutes of the Finance and Planning Committee of the Shelby County Health Care Corporation. You can pretty much pick a month at random:

"The Regional Medical Center: Net Loss for the month was $181,178 as compared with a budget of $228,118. Year-to-date net loss was $1,600,995 . . ."

The story gets gloomier as you read down the page. Perhaps the most revealing figure comes at the very bottom: "Cash and equivalents on hand were $12.779 million. Days cash on hand was 20.0, down from 20.3 last month."

Twenty days is not a lot of cover for an organization the size of the Med. Twenty days is not a lot of cover when so many of your patients can't pay. Twenty days is not a lot when you have no idea who will be coming through your door demanding to be treated, or what their needs will be.

"They want me to make cuts," she says. "But where do you start when everyone is overstretched? You can't trim thirteen million dollars."

It boils down to a simple question, a question that has not been resolved throughout the turbulent history of the United States: Who should pay for those who cannot pay for themselves? As Donelson put it, "Most days last week, between sixty and seventy inpatients who will not be able to pay their bills were treated at the Med. These patients have a lot in common. Most are unemployed. Most are not eligible for Tenncare [the state health subsidy program] and most are from Shelby County.

Most of them are also very sick. Last week their problems included a gunshot wound to the chest, a pregnancy outside the womb, multiple sclerosis, congestive heart failure and tuberculosis."

Donelson is very persuasive, if only because in this case the persuasion requires little more than a statement of the obvious: "At the end of March, the Med's cost of charity care and 'bad debt' was about $60 million for the first nine months of the fiscal year. . . . Free care is not free. It requires nurses, tests, equipment, transportation and physician time. . . ."

It requires money, public money.

Chapter 17

The Newborn Center

ACROSS THE ROAD from the current financial crisis, Dr. Sheldon Korones is carrying on regardless.

At the entrance hall to the Newborn Center he scrubs up and dons his gown. It's 4 P.M. and Dr. Korones is beginning his rounds. Much of the care is done by residents or the nurse practitioners (advanced care nurses, with master's degrees) and by a full support team of social workers, nutritionists and others, but every day Dr. Korones does the rounds, too.

"One of the reasons we do well," says Dr. Korones, "has to do with how we think about our work. When a child is born sick, or weighs only a pound, or when the child might die, for us this is not just a medical thing. It's a social thing, a family tragedy, and we treat it like one."

He is also proud that the Newborn Center is part of a teaching hospital. During his tenure, thirty-eight specialists in neonatal medicine have trained there, and he and others on his staff have published widely in scientific journals.

All of which must make him intimidating for the nurses?

"Oh, no," says Elizabeth Ivey, RN. "He's cute."

In the same way as a rattlesnake, perhaps?

"Don't be silly," says Elizabeth. She is a nurse practitioner, which is to say a nurse with a master's degree and many years' experience. She has pale skin and a wide, expressive mouth and today is wearing slightly dramatic glasses that give her the appearance of a trial lawyer, say, or a strict schoolteacher. This, of course, is precisely what she is not. She is one of those without whom, Dr. Korones says, "neither I nor this unit would survive."

Nor, one assumes, many of the babies in her care.

IT'S A BEAUTIFUL DAY and Elizabeth Ivey is, well, not bored exactly. Let's say she is less challenged. Two months of every year Elizabeth takes a break from the trials of the Newborn Center, the row upon row of tiny maybe-they'll-make-it babies in their incubators and comes "down" to work in the well-baby unit. Here children who need a day or two of observation, or whose mothers are being cared for in the hospital, are treated.

When I get there she is in consultation with two parents.

"Okay?" she says. "Nothing more than one hundred point four. She should never have a temperature more than that. Not one hundred and four, you hear. One hundred *point* four. Anything above that and you need to get someone to take a look at her."

The new parents are nodding their heads. They have that bemused expression I have seen—and no doubt had—in these circumstances. It is a mixture of disbelief and elated pride, with a big dose of fatigue thrown in.

"All right, then," Elizabeth says, ushering them out the door. "We'll see you next year!"

"Oh, God, no," says the mother.

"They all say that," says Elizabeth, coming over to where I am sitting. "But they'll be back, you watch."

She's carrying an armful of unruly files that threaten to spill out in all directions, but she manages—just—to get to the desk before dropping them.

"This is who we have today," she says. We're waiting for Dr. Korones to come and do his rounds and—unusually—he is late, which means we have a moment to talk. Elizabeth, whose praises Korones sings at the drop of a hat, has worked for—or with—him for sixteen years. "I qualified in 1986," she says, "and came straight here. I've been here all that time except when I went back to the University of Tennessee to do my master's and become a nurse practitioner."

Elizabeth in fact qualified in Texas at Baylor University ("Now, that's a whole other world. Those people wear cowboy boots to church") and worked for a while in Washington, D.C. ("I loved it. If I didn't have family here . . .").

Once qualified as a nurse practitioner, she came straight back to the Med. "There wasn't much demand elsewhere," she says, "and Dr. Korones was the first to realize we could be useful. He was the first to give us the kind of responsibility we have here."

There it is again. Every time I ask a nurse what it is they value about the Med, the answer comes back the same: They trust us. We have autonomy. We have freedom and responsibility. We're allowed to use the skills we have to do the job that needs doing. This is true of those who have worked only at the Med and those who have worked at other hospitals in Memphis and around the country. Even those who leave, like Peggy Simpson or Amy Delaney, are adamant that the one thing the Med does is give you that precious autonomy, the respect they think they deserve for the skills they have and the work they do.

"You know," says Elizabeth, "I think it is a fault of all of us generally to want money, rather than to be interested in personal and spiritual growth."

"You sound like Dr. Korones."

"Well, he is the man!"

We smile at the multiple ironies of this assessment and I watch Dr. Korones donning his robe on the other side of the glass doors. He's flirting—perhaps the word is too strong—being charming with the other nurses as someone does his bows, and then he comes through the doors. Between him and us are two rows of small beds, each with a baby on it. Nurses are comforting some. Some are moving their limbs, experimenting with their newfound freedom. But most are asleep and the room is quiet.

Dr. Korones greets Elizabeth and the two residents and sits down at the desk.

"Well, what have we today?"

What we have today is a story of a Memphis life, a life that seldom makes the headlines but that is all too real and too common and that passes, sometimes barely remarked, by the nurses at the Med. . . . A child born to a thirteen-year-old child who was raped by her stepfather—but he denies paternity. A child born to an HIV-positive mother who is being kept in the hospital and whose child, therefore, is staying in the hospital.

"Do we know what her home is like?" Korones asks.

"I can't even think of doing home visits," says Elizabeth as she shakes her head. "People like her don't stay around long enough in one place. They give a number when they're admitted to the hospital, but if you call that number the next day the person answering won't know where she is. It's hard. It's really hard."

They work through the cases. Sometimes Elizabeth gives a description of the case history; sometimes it falls to the two residents. It is clear that Elizabeth has status in this, and she and Korones tease the residents a little.

"Ooh, didn't she use the right word!" exclaims Elizabeth when the resident avoids using "stable" to describe a patient who is "doing nicely."

"I should hope so," says Korones, for whom a pet theme is that "the most stable patient is a dead one."

BUT THE REAL ISSUE for today is the high incidence of Group B streptococcus, which over the past decade has become recognized as the number-one cause of life-threatening infections in newborn babies. It is more common than more commonly known diseases like rubella. It's a field of study in which Korones has become nationally known, but what interests me is the extent to which he implicitly trusts Elizabeth's judgments in this matter.

The debate works something like this: since GBS (aka Bstrep) is little known, many women are not screened for it during their prenatal care. And many patients at the Med, of course, have little or no prenatal care at all. The policy at the Med is to screen all mothers and children after birth—which is one reason why they're kept in for twenty-four hours, and in a little over 90 percent of cases, if GBS is present, it will manifest itself in the first twenty-four hours.

If so, it is easily treated with penicillin. The problem is what to do if it has not been detected before the child is born, and what to do if the status of mother and child is "unknown."

"We're getting a lot of unknowns," says Elizabeth. "Say we get seven patients in tonight. Five of those will have had inadequate prenatal care. So those five will be 'unknown.' And so what happens is we have to keep them in an additional twenty-four hours to be safe. Every day the unknowns and the 'inadequates' [she means inadequately screened] exceed the 'knowns' and the 'adequates.'"

"Can you give me a survey?" says Korones.

"I can."

"Thank you."

"You're very welcome."

THEY WORK THEIR WAY through the thirty-one patients on today's roster. From time to time Korones scratches comments on the patient record, but more often he approves what Elizabeth or the residents have already written.

The session breaks up.

"Any other problems?" says Dr. Korones.

"Only the plague."

And when he has gone, Elizabeth runs through the list with the residents, making sure they have understood what needs to be done for the next twenty-four hours.

"I ALWAYS WANTED to be a nurse," she tells me. "My mother always knew I would be a nurse. I always took care of everyone. All my pet animals, you know, all my stuffed toys? Well, when I was a kid they all needed their chests listened to all the time."

"You get on well with Dr. Korones?" I ask disingenuously.

"For me it is such a privilege to work with him," she says, but then she rethinks this. "We're actually very different," she says. "I am a Republican with a capital R. I believe in all the basic Republican ideals: the right to own a business, the freedom to make money and to look after your family. But to Dr. Korones the idea that health care can be a business is anathema. He really believes that is what gets in the way of people getting the care they need."

"So how do you reconcile this?"

"The party is not the problem," she says, still thinking of her capital R. "I believe the party wants to care. The difficulty is how you deliver that."

"And who pays for those who can't pay for themselves?"

"Can't, or won't?" she says, which is pretty much the nub of the matter, whether it is debated in passing over a cup of coffee, or is at the end of several days of horse-trading at the state budget committee. The question of who pays—and to whom—drives these debates as surely as the sun drives the seasons, and for almost everyone the answer is: not me.

On other matters Elizabeth has what you might describe as "compassionate conservative" views. "Dads are hard to come by in our demographic. They all have them—but they're not real involved." Or: "They can refuse to have an HIV test when they come in or during their antenatal care. But I'm not sure that's right. If we don't test them, we can't treat it. It's a moral thing, you know? What about mother-to-child transmission?"

ELIZABETH TAKES ME on a tour of the babies and I recall those I have seen previously in the intensive care incubators of the Newborn Center. The smallest she has seen survive is a 400-gram baby—"not unscathed, but still a great child for someone to have." She has seen many die.

"People ask me how I can work here, where these babies are so sick. I can because many of them get better. And you never know which one is going to 'be a gunner.' Do you know that expression?"

I confess that I don't.

"You know, be the one that is game for everything, the one that will survive no matter what the odds. Some kids just have it in them, and for me—that's amazing."

"And you see them here?"

"We see them all here. This is the Med, you know."

CHAPTER 18

Life Goes On

"NURSE, NURSE," says the patient in delivery room 3 at the Rout Center for Women and Newborns. "Could you rub my stomach?" Mercedita Neal's eyes crinkle, which I take to mean that she is smiling beneath her surgical mask.

"Rub it?"

"Yeah, please."

"Well now, honey, you've got a free hand there. Why don't *you* rub it?"

But Mercy, a registered nurse, goes over anyway and rubs the patient's stomach. It is unlikely the patient can feel much—no doubt the source of the request—because the epidural is just about to take effect and in ten minutes' time the surgeons will make the incision through which they will deliver her first baby.

The father is looking on in bemusement. "Her first?" I asked him as we got dressed a few minutes before.

"Uh-huh," he said, and then, lest I get the wrong impression, he added, "My seventh."

"It's not elective," said the nurse manager. "But she's not changing, so we're going to do a C-section."

"I DON'T LIKE TO WATCH," the father-to-be (for the seventh time) added as we entered the delivery room and he took up a position next to his partner's head and held briefly the hand with which she was now rubbing her numb stomach.

I have witnessed the vaginal deliveries of my three children, but this is the first time I have seen a C-section. The surgeons make the first incision at 5:13 P.M. By 5:25 it's pretty much all over. The baby is born, cleaned, weighed, tagged, swaddled and handed over to its parents. There is nothing more to do except "sew her up and move her out"—except for the small matter of the swabs.

"Five, six, seven, eight . . ." Mercy counts.

"Seventeen, eighteen, nineteen . . ." responds the scrub nurse.

They're one short and the count starts again. This time they get the correct number. One fell out of view beneath the bed.

"We're good," says Mercy, and the resident starts to stitch.

"Are we through?" says the mother.

"We are so almost through," comes the response.

THE FATHER AND I leave at the same time.

"I gotta get something to eat," he says, with the air of a man who, despite himself, has been through something intense and draining.

❂

LATER I CAUGHT UP with Mercy, who originally came from the Philippines. Her name was mentioned in the context of a discussion of recruiting problems and the nursing shortage. Recently the Med has been looking outside the United States for its nurses. Other hospitals go much further. An article in *The New York Times* talks about "binge-hiring" in countries like India and the Philippines.

It wasn't quite like that for Mercy.

She was born in 1959 on Camiguin, a small island north of Mindanao in the Philippines. I had spent some time in Mindanao and could still dredge up two or three words of Tagalog, which meant that we instantly had some common ground. "You should come and see my house," said Mercy. "Come and see what the American dream can be. Because if you know Mindanao, you know where I'm coming from."

Mindanao is the largest island in the Filipino archipelago, home to the towering Mount Apo. When I was there a decade before, we spent some time filming a group of indigenous people who were slowly, surely, being dispossessed of their land and their livelihoods by the encroaching needs of "lowland" peasant farmers. I remember the crowded backstreets of Davao City and the tiny stalls selling candles, matches, cooking oil and machetes high on the slopes of a sleeping volcano.

It is a long way from the broad tree-lined avenues off Overton Park in midtown Memphis where I go to visit Mercy and her version of the American dream. From the teasing tone in her voice I was not sure whether Mercy meant for me to take her comment seriously. One look at the house and I know she does. It's a large brick building on a half-acre lot in a very smart part of town.

"So my father didn't want me to do nursing," she says. "He was a businessman and he thought I should go into business. But I knew that nursing was a way to get to America, and, like all Filipinos, what I wanted more than anything was to come here."

Mercy graduated in 1981 from South Western University, Cebu City. For three long years—"long, hard years"—she worked in the rural areas of Camiguin as a public health nurse. And then in 1984 she took a deep breath and—using all her savings—bought a plane ticket to America. It took a while to pass some more exams and get her license, but eventually she did. These, too, were hard years "living in a small room, not talking to anyone," but in 1987 she got a position in the birth unit at the Med. And she's been there ever since.

Mercy's view of America is not necessarily what I would have expected from someone whose background was working in the poorest rural areas of the poorest part of the Philippines.

"I had never seen anything like it," she says. "All these undersized babies. All these infections. All these complications. Where I came from every birth was routine. Here every birth is complicated. Why is that? How can this be in a place that has so much money? All these sick people? That's what I was thinking. Now I understand a little more, but still, here at the Med, I see things I would never have believed."

What Mercy is talking about is the catalog of ill health associated with being poor and urban in America. Drugs, malnutrition, lack of education, lack of health care, no prenatal care, HIV.

Although she had made it to America, and although she found work, her first experiences were not quite the American Dream Mercy had in mind. It was too hard. People were too sick. After five years at the Med she and a friend were planning to travel. With their licenses and their Med experience they would be able to pick up work wherever they went. It would be fun.

Except that she met her husband, a banker. "We dated for five years. He wanted to get married earlier," she tells me, "but I said no. I wanted to be sure that he understood where I was coming from. I wanted to be sure he knew me inside and out. You know, like I was paying for my brothers to go through school. This isn't just a money thing. This is about obligations on both sides."

Her husband survived this "Mercy test" and in 1996 they married. They now have one son and this large house in a smart part of midtown Memphis.

"But I remember," says Mercy. "I'm becoming American, but I don't let myself forget. When I was a nurse in the Philippines I had only one pair of shoes. For four years! Can you believe it? Now I keep that pair of shoes to remind myself."

"What does it mean to be American?" I ask. We're both laughing but her answer is serious.

"What I learn from my husband. It is easier to buy a new TV than to repair the old one. In the Third World you learn how to wait, to be patient. Here I am like everyone else. I want everything quicker. That's the way here. Run, run, run."

Michael, her son, is just starting to walk. "He hasn't been home yet," she says. "We'll go soon. I'm going to take him a lot because it will be good for him to see another part of the world."

We sit and sip water and enjoy the air-conditioned quiet of her house.

"When I go home," she says, "all my friends say, 'Oh, you're doing good.' They want to come to America and be my maid. That's how good I'm doing."

So good her friends want to be her maid.

"And now I've got my baby." She tells me they had some difficulty getting pregnant. She wasn't sure they could have a baby. But when they did, there was only one place she was going.

"Oh, the Med," she says. "Definitely. I had my own team. No residents, only staff doctors. Nurses I know." She remembers all the details. Operating room 2. Suite 6. November 1, 2001, "just after Halloween."

"It was so smooth," she says. "No problems, no pain. It was how it should be."

NINETEEN MONTHS LATER I watched another child being born. This, too, was a relatively simple affair, a C-section without complications.

"I wish they were all like that," says Trina Ellis, RN. She's just come off the phone with a prospective patient and it is clear that she has conversations like this too often for her liking.

"You say your last period was in May? And you've done a pregnancy test? And it was positive. You are pregnant? Okay, then you should not be bleeding. No. No, not like that."

They agree that the patient will "come on in."

"But you've got to be pregnant, you hear? If you aren't pregnant they'll send you to the emergency room. So make sure you bring that test proof with you, okay?"

Trina hangs up and turns to me with a sigh.

"People don't know a lot," she says, "about how their bodies work. There's so much basic stuff that they just don't understand."

Trina is twenty-nine and works in the assessment unit of the birthing place at the Med. She's been there three years and wouldn't have it any other way. "I love this place," she says. "This is where I was born."

At that moment one of the resident physicians calls her away to "chaperone" him as he works with a woman in the early stages of labor. While I wait for her return I see a notice from security taped to the wall at the nurses' station: it concerns an "African-American woman, about 5'3", 180 lbs, 28 years old" who has visited several hospitals in the area recently, posing as a charity worker and saying her organization wants to offer free diapers and other materials to new mothers.

But—so reads the notice—she "fits the profile of an abductor." I reflect that even here, far from the drama and violence of the trauma ward, hospitals are semipublic spaces. The ID card I have allows me to walk through doors marked "Authorized," but other members of the public use their own methods to get in. All the nurses have stories about people who come to the Med—stray men walking down corridors, homeless people looking for shelter, gangsters looking for the body of a deceased gang member.

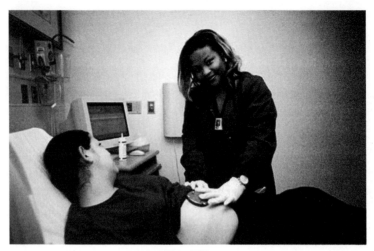

Trina Ellis

"We have to be aware," says Trina. "Like you see here—all the rooms are numbers with letters rather than just numbers. That's because the rooms in delivery are only numbered. And one time this man came in looking for his wife. He'd been told she was in room eight or nine or whatever. So he goes to room eight and sticks his head in the door and all he can see is a patient in labor. And he says, 'Keisha, is that you? What happened to your butt? That don't look like your butt!'

"And this poor woman is contracting while some guy is being rude about her butt, because of course Keisha is in room eight in the delivery section, not here. So we have to be careful."

Trina has her life in order. She has two children of her own—born at Baptist rather than the Med because that's where her husband's health insurance sent them—and doesn't plan to have any more. "You know, what my husband says is kids are real expensive. And you want to give them everything you can, so, no, I don't think we will have any more." She graduated in May 2003 and has worked at the Med ever since, although she did have stints as a nursing extern at both Baptist and Methodist. And things are going "good, pretty good. Although if I got pregnant again," she says, "I would come to the Med. The standard of care here is really exceptional. Whenever people come here they're always surprised at how good it is. 'Cause pretty is not always good."

I look around the wards, which are functional and clean, but not exactly pretty.

"There's a lot of money in nursing," she says. "But you have to go out and get it. You have to do the work. Here I make fifty thousand a year, no problem. Maybe a little more, depending on how hard I work." (At the moment Trina does seven twelve-hour shifts every fortnight.) "I could make more if I went and did agency work, but the trouble with agency is you're never part of a team. You're on your own. I like to be part of the team here.

"It's the permanent staff that make the system work."

Other nurses in the room agree.

"The thing is," says one, "most of us don't really do this job for the money—but at the same time none of us are suffering at the Med."

"It's a dream job," says Trina. "But now I want to get into a nurse practitioner program. As an FNP I can make seventy or eighty thousand, no problem. That would be good."

She has plans in place and has identified a small school in Mississippi where she can do it. "It's tailored to each person," she says, "and takes twelve months. But it means I can work here and do my school and still see my family. Neat, huh?"

There is a sense of satisfaction in all this missing from the trauma ward, where nurses live more on the edge. The nurses in labor and delivery see perhaps as many problematic cases, but the unit attracts people who are in it for the long haul, people for whom it is a dream job.

"But I look at these people," says Trina, "and I wonder about their lives. I see people every day who don't take care of their bodies. They don't have insurance or they don't have transport and so they're pregnant, but while they're pregnant they're not getting any care.

"Or sometimes they're poor but they come in here with their nails done and their Gucci bags—and no health care. They have money, but they're not using it appropriately."

TRINA AND NURSES like her are accurate barometers of class and race in a city like Memphis. She, for example, knows about the growth of the city's Hispanic population, not from reading reports or studying it at college but because these are the people who walk through the door.

"I'm having to learn some Spanish," she says with a smile. "¿Mucho dolor?" And then she laughs as she imitates a mother's melodramatic "¡Sí, sí-í-í! Mucho dolor."

But she also knows that poor Memphis is represented in her wards by young black mothers, like the ten-year-old child who was delivered by C-section the week before. "We had to oper-ate because there was clear fetal distress. And so for this kid it is just trauma piled on trauma. The baby didn't make it, but that was going to happen anyway."

"The heartbreaking part is the pattern."

This last comment is not from Trina Ellis but from Elizabeth Ivey, RN, who works with Dr. Korones upstairs in the Newborn Center of which he is so proud. It is Elizabeth and her colleagues who care for and ensure the survival of so many babies of—how does one put this?—high-risk pregnancies.

"The heartbreaking part is the pattern," she told me earlier in the day. "You see a mom and she's got a six-hundred- or seven-hundred-gram baby and you realize that you saw her a year or two years ago. And you're trying to remember, did that one make it?

"But you can't ask and you just have to deal with her because here she is again, like nothing has gotten better."

PART 4

Summer

CHAPTER 19

Morphine and Jelly Babies

It's a smallish room in the middle of an ugly part of town, where Union meets Interstate 280. A few hundred yards away the neon lights of Anywhere, U.S.A.—Burger King, Walgreens, Texaco—shine through the gathering gloom. Behind me is a desolate stretch of inner-city low-income housing interspersed with vacant lots and run-down churches. There's a smell of microwaved food in the room; in one corner the television is tuned to a local news station. Today there is only one item of local news: the weather, which is bad. There are tornado warnings in twelve counties and things are expected to get worse.

I am a little tired and I find myself studying a note pinned to the wall. It has today's date and the beginning of what looks like a shopping list: Jelly Babies, milk, morphine . . . There's another list next to it of the "ten most wanted." Domino's. TCBY. Krystal's . . .

It is only after some moments of looking intently at the first list that I think to ask what it means.

"It's our shopping list," says Barbara Wells, RN. "Molly's going out in a minute to get some food, but we also need more morphine."

"And Jelly Babies," yells Teresa Fulwood, RN, from the back. "Don't forget my Jelly Babies."

I am at the helicopter base for Hospital Wing, the helicopter that services the four main hospitals in central Memphis. The service is jointly owned by the four hospitals but it is the nature of the patient load—and the nature of the area—that roughly half the people picked up by Wing are taken to the Med. Many are "transfers" from one hospital to another, but almost all of the "scene flights"—for motor vehicle accidents and shootings— involve taking patients to the Med. It's Dennis's phrase again. The Med's where they take you . . . if you're all messed up in Memphis.

It was at Hospital Wing that Sharon Lucus worked before going back to school to become a nurse anesthetist, and it is here that many nurses would like to work.

"We don't have a problem recruiting," says Barbara, "and once nurses are here they tend to stay for a long time."

"Why?"

Without any observable irony, it is Molly Barry, RN, who calls out her answer. "Flight nursing is as high as you can go," she says, "at least in a staff position. There's no place your skills are going to be tested more. There's no place you count for more. In this it's what you know, what your skills are, that determines everything."

"None of us are under thirty," says Barbara. "We need to know too much. We have to make difficult decisions and we need to get it right." Barbara got married at eighteen and divorced at twenty-eight. Now forty-eight, she has been a nurse for twenty-eight years. She spent eleven of those in the trauma unit, the past seventeen at Hospital Wing. "I wouldn't change it for anything," she says. Like other nurses, she values the autonomy, but also the schedule. Working two twenty-four-hour shifts a week leaves her plenty of time for the pet cemetery and cremation business she runs in Millington, north of Memphis.

Hospital Wing works like this: there are three helicopters, two of which are in service at any one time, and there are sixteen nurses, each of whom works two twenty-four-hour shifts a week. Allowing for holidays and sick leave, this means that there are four nurses on duty at any one time, two per helicopter.

By this time Barbara has roused me from my fatigue and taken me through the hangar where all three helicopters have been brought in. There are tornado warnings, and Phil Scruggs, the chief pilot, is not about to risk the aircraft in that kind of weather.

The Eurocopter AS35 B3s are all the same and are a surprisingly tight fit. "They've got to be small," Barbara explains, "to get into the places we need to get to."

Everything they might need has its place. The stretcher cot is on the port side, the pilot on the right starboard. The stretcher slides through a door and into a tightly fitting rack. Behind the pilot the nurses sit on a small bench. The one next to the patient takes care of the medical matters. The other is in communication with the hospital, warning them what's coming. I've spent enough time in the shock trauma unit now to know the other half of that equation. The "MVA by air, five minutes" that comes in on Kerry's radio comes via Medcom from these nurses. I can easily picture the activity and tension in the trauma area.

"Are you ever in danger?" I ask. I have visions of the chopper flying through the night to the scene of an attempted homicide. I can imagine the sirens and the officers with guns drawn. I can see the screaming neighbors and the gunman sweating nervously. I can—

Molly interrupts my television-inspired reverie.

"Sometimes," she says. "Sometimes. We try not to land unless we know the scene is safe. We'll be on the radio the whole time asking, 'Is it safe, is it safe?' And normally we won't be dispatched if it's not. But sometimes it happens. Maybe we get there and the gunman has escaped. Once I was doing CPR on a kid who had been shot. He had seven bullet wounds. And the guy who shot him has another bullet wound. And it's a political choice, you know. I have to decide who goes with us. And then there were police all around and then the officer says, 'Get going. Now.' You know, like, 'NOW!' And there's all these other people from the project coming now. Friends of the bad guy and so on. So we move out with the kid and as I run back to the chopper all I can hear is this black guy saying, 'That white bitch is gonna let him die.'

"But those are the exceptions. Mostly the difficult part is dealing with the public and still getting done what needs to be done. If you're trying to intubate a patient and someone is yelling at you to get him to the hospital . . ."

"Intubating is the worst," agrees Jan Weathered, RN.

"There's all that blood and mess and you've got to make sure you get the tube in the right place. You don't want it going into the patient's stomach."

And do they ever feel like quitting?

Both shake their heads.

"No. No," says Tonya March, RN. "The worst was . . . I can tell you the date, July third, 1999. We did seventeen flights in a twenty-four-hour shift and I was so tired I thought I was going to pass out. And they were all long flights."

She shakes her head at the memories.

"But quit? Never."

"Boy, it's a hot one," Tonya says. "Man!"

It's early July and Memphis is sweltering. Sweat drips off me the moment I step outside. There is no wind. The previous day there was a brief thunderstorm but it hardly cooled things at all. The forecast is for more of the same, only hotter.

"Must be Barbara firing up the bakery," someone jokes, a mischievous reference to Barbara Wells's other job as proprietor and part-time manager of her pet cemetery and crematorium.

"Hot days are never good," says Tonya, coming in from a flight. We shake hands and already she's asking, "How does my hair look?"

"You having a blond moment?" Jan teases her.

"Sorry, I was." Tonya grins. "I have them. I have blond moments."

"She's blond," Jan explains, "but she's not *a blonde*. You can't

Tonya March

work here and be a blonde." The nurses at Hospital Wing are not, of course, wearing scrubs. Their colors are claret and navy and they wear either overalls or shirts and heavy cotton trousers. I watch Barbara as she searches her pockets for a pen. It becomes almost mesmerizing as she works her way through the five, no, ten, no, fifteen pockets in her overalls.

THE RED TELEPHONE on the desk remains beatifically quiet and we have time to relax in the air-conditioning and talk. Tonya interests me because she, too, is leaving nursing—to become a lawyer.

"I graduate in December," she says, "and sit my bar exam in February. The results come through in May. I'll be here a little after that, I guess. Maybe until next summer."

Tonya took up the law because the legal and ethical aspects of her work as a nurse fascinated her. It's taken nearly five years, but she's pleased to have stuck with it—and even more pleased to have been able to hold down a full-time job at the same time. Like many nurses, she knows that working twenty-four-hour shifts gives her a freedom she could never have in more prosaic jobs. And the pay is good, which is something of a problem for Tonya (and a surprise for me).

"A problem?" I ask.

"Uh-huh. With extra shifts I make something over fifty-five thousand as a nurse," she replies. "But the starting salary for an attorney is forty-two thousand."

I can't quite believe her, but when I check later I find that the Tennessee Attorney General's Office has some attorneys on a starting salary of $37,000, although, of course, there are private sector firms that pay considerably more. It does reinforce the point, though, that nurses are well paid and have commensurate benefits. And no one is laying them off. Of all the professions, particularly in the current climate, nursing appears to be one of the least vulnerable to changes in the economy.

WE TAKE OFF, heading west, but soon swing south. Tonya's partner on this shift is Cindi Bailey, RN. She is next to the stretcher, Tonya next to the window. I'm sandwiched in between. Our pilot for this flight is David Childress, who has been flying helicopters for thirty-five years. Below me Memphis takes shape as it did the first time from the window of my airplane seat. In the distance I can see the river and the Pyramid, and below me the Temple of Deliverance, Church of God in Christ, passes. Its vast parking lot is empty now, but even from this altitude the hexagonal building is impressive.

We pick up the flight path heading south along the route of Interstate 55. As we fly, Cindi is on the airwaves talking to Medcom.

"What do we know?" she asks.

"Single male," comes the reply. "He was doing wheelies on his motorbike and it flipped."

Cindi and Tonya raise their eyebrows as if to say, "Men!"

"Possible head injuries," says the man at Medcom.

"Anything else?"

"That's all I got."

"Okay."

Within minutes we're over Whitehaven, the commuter-and-shopping-mall town just north of the Mississippi state line. David has the coordinates given by the EMT, but they're slightly off. Fortunately we "have visibility" and the flashing police lights and the fire engine tell us where to go.

"I got them," says David.

"Ideally we want two hundred feet by two hundred feet to land," says Tonya. "But if we've only got a hundred we can do it."

"If the weather's good."

Our conversation is interrupted because we're on the ground in a quiet residential street and Tonya is out the door and running. I want to know how long it will take them to get the patient back to the Med. I'm slightly skeptical of the whole chopper service. How much difference can it make? Earlier one of the nurses told me that they are required to be "in the air" within five minutes of a call from Medcom. There are obviously no set requirements for the other end—but how quick will it be?

In this case the patient is already in an ambulance. The task is to get him out, transfer him to the helicopter stretcher and get him to the hospital. The Medcom flight record tells the story best:

> Radio call time: 10:31
> Wing requested: 10:33
> Dispatch time: 10:35
> Liftoff: 10:38
> On-scene time: 10:45
> Transport time: 10:56
> Arrival time: 11:02

This is a reasonably routine flight. The patient is not entirely cooperative, but neither is he violent. He is, in the jargon, only A&O x 1, meaning he knows the date but cannot recall his name or his location. He has severe abrasions down one side of his body and apparent bruising on his head, despite having worn a helmet. He tries to fight the nurses a little, and tries to sit up, a common reaction to concussion. Both Cindi and Tonya are firm.

"Do not do that, sir," says Cindi. "Do not do that. Now we're going to strap you in, sir. Yes, your arms, too. We do not want you opening the helicopter door."

"Hold still," says Tonya, and he does.

In those few short minutes on the return flight to the landing pad on the fifth floor above Shock Trauma, Tonya finds time to answer some more of my questions. The patient is quiet and stable—that word again—and Cindi is doing the "paperwork" on strips of tape stuck on her uniform trousers for that purpose.

Since Tonya is going to be a lawyer, I ask her the obvious question. "Do you ever get sued?"

She laughs at my naïveté. "You better believe it," she says. "Just recently a guy called me at work. 'Is that Tonya March?' he says. I tell him it is. And then the doorbell rings. I go the door and there's this guy on his cell phone waiting to serve a subpoena on me."

Mostly civil suits involving nurses are not personal. Mostly they're named as John Doe or Jane Doe in personal injury cases against the hospital(s). And quite frequently they are called on to give depositions or sign affidavits relating to what they have seen at a "scene." She has a case dating back as far as 1998 still waiting to come to court. Earlier that day Peggy Simpson said much the same thing of her work in Burn. "The only bit that stays is the litigation. The Med's lawyers have discovered that I know an awful lot about burns and so I'm helping them with a case. Still."

We touch down.

I go with Cindi, who takes the patient into the shock trauma unit. Tonya will head back to Hospital Wing to restock the aircraft and do the paperwork. Later someone will come to fetch Cindi.

"Don't forget my tickets for Wimbledon," she says, in refer-

ence to a running joke between us. Tonya and Jan tend to take
vacations together. "We want to go to Wimbledon," they said.

I smile, my mind still preoccupied with the efficiency of the
helicopter trip. Tonya sees the look on my face.

"Sorry," she says, "that was a blond moment."

HALF AN HOUR LATER Jan Weathered comes in from another
flight, also with someone who crashed his motorcycle.

"You got to love it," she says, "the way vomit just brings
people closer together. This guy just threw up all over my aircraft." He threw up over her as well, and there is blood and
vomit on her shirt and trousers.

I thought it was touching that she worried more about the
aircraft than herself.

"But hey, this is the Med," she says.

Chapter 20

Calling Elvis

The traffic on I-240 was jammed up, but it didn't take long to find out why. This time it was a small pileup—just three cars—big enough to mean that the traffic had to be squeezed into a single lane. This was in June and as I drove past I, like everyone else, "rubbernecked" the accident. The police and the ambulances were there already, lights flashing. I couldn't see any patients but I noted an ambulance license plate just for interest. I wondered whether I would get to the Med before it did. It did not, for a moment, occur to me that the patients would be taken anywhere else. It was round about then that I began to feel I had been there too long.

As it happened I made it to the Med and was walking in the entrance to Trauma just as the ambulance pulled up. I took a moment to watch the well-rehearsed routine as the patient was wheeled in through the electronic doors and into the assessment room.

What happens is that the nurses and physicians have been

forewarned. The Medcom operatives will have put in a radio call saying, "Female, MVA by land, seven minutes," and people know what to expect. En route the ambulance crew will have given as much advance notice of injuries as possible. Ideally there will be no surprises. In Shock Trauma they will try to stabilize the patient. It is only later, should it be necessary, that they will show up in the trauma operating rooms.

"AN OPERATION CAN take a long time," says Lynda Pulley, RN. She's the nurse supervisor for Trauma OR. "Twelve hours is not unusual. And so we have to have something to relieve the tension. You can't be serious the whole time. And, besides, the physicians love it."

The "it" Lynda is referring to is the habit the nurses have in the trauma operating rooms (TOR) of playing Elvis Presley songs, sometimes very loud.

" 'Blue Suede Shoes' is a favorite," she says. "It breaks the monotony nicely.

"But not if someone is dying," she adds. "That wouldn't be right."

Not many people die in OR, another nurse told me. "Someone looks like dying, they do everything they can to get him out of there before it happens. If someone dies in OR, the family are going to want to know the details. If someone dies in a hospital after an accident—well, these things happen."

I am in Lynda Pulley's office in the trauma OR unit of the Elvis Presley Memorial Trauma Center at the Med and I am wondering whether I should mention this. I decide not to, because Lynda, the nurse manager for the unit, appears to take it very seriously indeed. Every available space in her office is covered by images of the man. Posters, cards, fridge magnets, dolls, key rings . . . the flotsam of the Elvis industry is crawling across her desk and up her walls. In one corner there's a giant cardboard cutout of the man. There are cartoons and drawings, too, and Lynda smiles to see me looking at a warning on her chair: "Elvis Fans Parking Only: Violators will be all shook up." But in the face of such enthusiasm it is hard not to have some doubts. "Fifty million fans can't be wrong" . . . can they?

Lynda smiles when I ask her about the wall outside Trauma ICU. "We call it the 'wailing wall,'" she says. "The fans come by and they like to pose and have their photos taken and so on. And sometimes they just burst into tears."

"But you're a fan?" I ask.

She shrugs. "Who isn't?" Lynda joined the trauma unit at the Med twenty years ago, before it was named for its eponymous hero. "I wouldn't work anywhere else," she says, "and I'm not going to move unless they make me."

I'm about to ask why, but she is already answering me.

"For a start I wouldn't get paid any more. I've been here twenty years. I'm on a pretty good rate. Mind you, that's true of most of the nurses in this unit. The average age here is forty-eight, I think. These are very experienced, very competent nurses. And we aren't going anywhere. We do two twenty-four-hour shifts, which means a lot of us can do extra at other hospitals if we need to.

"But even without that, I wouldn't go anywhere else. I always wanted to be where the action is, and in Memphis, this is it. You turn on the news in this town and there's been an accident or something? Sooner or later you're going to see a reporter standing outside the Med, right outside that door there."

THERE ARE NO REPORTERS one Thursday in June when I walk into the OR section of the trauma unit. There were earlier in the week. A light aircraft "flipped" on landing at Memphis International Airport and killed two passengers, wounding two others. Within minutes of the story's emerging, there were television crews on the steps of the Med, before the injured had arrived even. It's a shorter drive from the TV station than from the airport and the crews were never in any doubt as to where the injured would be taken.

I go through the swing doors into Trauma and pretty soon I'm standing at the nurses' station. From behind glass doors I can just hear the sound of music playing. The nurse at the station is called Elvis—"Not for the obvious reason," she tells me—and I ask where I can find Becky Laster, RN. Elvis nods at a whirling blue dervish coming through the door.

"That's her."

"Hold still!" says the vision in blue. "Don't move!"

Becky is dressed in full OR gear, including scrubs, mask, surgical cap and gloves. All I can see of her is her eyes, gleaming with intent.

"We've got a fly situation," she says through her mask. "And if there's one thing we do *not* want it is a fly." At this moment I am partially clothed in my gown and mask, almost ready to be allowed into OR. We're in the antechamber that leads through

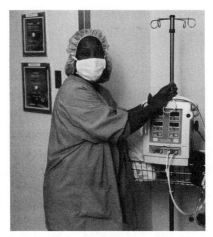

Becky Laster

automatic doors to the four operating rooms of the trauma unit. I continue to dress but Becky yells again.

"Hold still!"

I hold still and watch as in a flurry of rustling blue she nails the fly against the wall, right next to a poster spelling out "Your Rights as a Patient." She puts it and her gloves in a disposal unit and then turns to shake my hand. Our introduction doesn't last long.

"You the man? I heard about you. Got to get back," she says, and (fully washed and clothed again) she leads me through to the suite of operating rooms. "We're dealing with a messed-up arm in there."

I recognize the arm. It belongs to a motorcyclist I saw brought into Shock Trauma the day before. According to the EMT I spoke to, the driver hit something on the road, maybe a wet patch, careened off the road and smacked into a tree. The bike was a write-off, but the rider doesn't seem to be in too bad shape ... except for his arm. Like so many patients, he was taken straight to the Med.

Once assessed, the patient disappeared into the privacy of his own "bay." But now I recognize the arm as soon as I see it, the skin protruding in all the wrong places.

For this operation Becky is "circulating" as opposed to "scrub" nurse. The scrub nurse is there to support the surgeons. She or he is the one you see on TV holding out the scalpel or the suture a nanosecond before the surgeon asks for it. The circulating nurse is making notes, fetching additional supplies, keeping in touch with the real world outside. Operations can take a long time, and while the surgeons and the scrub nurse work, Becky and I have time to talk.

Becky is forty-nine. I haven't yet seen her face, but later I discover she looks like Whoopi Goldberg's older sister, the one who got a proper job instead of messing about in comedy clubs. She's been at the Med for just over four years, having previously worked for eighteen years at St. Joseph's Hospital not too far away.

"But it closed," she says. "This was the obvious place to come.

"Have you seen his arm?" she adds.

I move over to see his arm. As is common in operating room procedure, the patient's head is hidden behind blue sheeting and only the part of the body the surgeons are working on is visible. In this case the arm is open from below the elbow to his hand. The scale and complexity of the fractures are evident in the X-rays displayed on the viewing panel on the wall. It looks like a mess. We watch in silence as the surgeons work.

An hour passes.

"Looks like it'll be a long one," says Becky before taking me through some of the jargon: BBFA means "both bone fore-arm." ORIF means "open reduction internal fixation" ("They put a plate in, right?"). On the carding system she has details of the next case for this OR. It involves more orthopedic work on a patient's leg.

"So what I got to do is make sure supply sends up all the stuff we need for the next one."

She shows me where the surgeons have written what they anticipate they will need—and then she shows me the things she has asked for even though they haven't, because long experience has taught her what to expect.

"It's the same with time. You see there—that's how long the physician thinks it will take. He says four hours. Trust me, we'll be lucky to be out of there in eight."

For the operation on the motorcyclist's arm the estimate was five hours. Becky changed it to seven. We're at eight hours and counting when she looks at her watch (which is a Med watch, complete with insignia). The surgeons have begun the final stitching of the arm.

"Time to let his family know. They'll be real anxious sitting out there. I like to keep them updated on how things are going."

But the family, who had been in the waiting room, have gone to find something to eat, so Becky and I have some more time to talk.

"You like this?" I ask. It's not that I'm squeamish, exactly, but neither do I find the blood-and-chrome aesthetic of the operating theater particularly alluring.

"I've worked other places," Becky says. "I came up the long route. I was an LPN before I became a nurse. And I did some psychiatric nursing, some OB, some ICU. But this here is my calling. What I like about this is you have only got one patient at a time. On the floor you're maybe looking after ten patients. In Shock Trauma if someone goes into arrest you have to drop everything and run. Here you can take the time it needs and do everything right. I like that."

"Nice answer," says Frank, the X-ray technician, who has been listening in.

"You betcha," says Becky. "I should be on TV."

A FEW MINUTES LATER I go with Becky as she wheels the patient out of the OR and into his room in the intensive care unit.

"Now I gotta find his family," she says. "The worst thing for anyone is not knowing. They have a right to know."

It is not particularly the job of the nurse to dig out a patient's family and let them know what is happening. And nurses have to be careful what they say. They do not want to tread on any surgeon's toes. They do not want to give answers to medical questions that should more properly be answered by a physician. But what these nurses do understand is that not knowing is invariably worse than knowing, and uncertainty is debilitating. So Becky finds the family members out on the steps of the Med, watching the traffic ease its way up Jefferson Avenue.

"He's going to be okay," she says. "I think things went okay. We'll have to see how it turns out. You can go see him in maybe an hour, okay?"

In the quiet of the OR Becky tells me a little about herself. "You can call me Becky," she says, "except when I'm in uniform. Then you can call me Major."

Becky is a member—a ranking member—of the army reserve and spends at least one weekend a month in training camps. She likes the life and has been in the army reserve since 1977.

"Why did you join?"

"Same reason as everyone else. I was young enough and stupid enough. And they were offering to pay for my training. But it's been good for me. They've been good to me."

She has not yet served in the Gulf—her only foreign posting was a brief goodwill mission to El Salvador—but she expects to be called up at some point.

And her rank?

"Well, you know what they say," she says. "'Blank' rolls downhill." I'm touched by her girlish modesty in refusing to swear, at least for the record. "Rank has its privileges," she continues. "So here I can do all that 'yes, Doctor; no, Doctor' stuff."

As it happens, Becky's days in the military are nearly over. Within weeks she'll have her twenty years and be able to seek an honorable discharge. By the time I make my final visit to the Med, she has done that.

"Will you miss it?" I ask.

"No way," she replies. "Why would I miss it?" She gestures at the OR area. "Why would I miss it when I've got this?" At first I think she is joking, but I watch her face and I realize she isn't. "This" is not just a hospital; it is a community of like-minded—or mostly like-minded—people, and what Becky has is not just the community but a sense of belonging and—if this is the word—the comradeship that comes from working long, intensive hours together.

CHAPTER 21

Self-Inflicted Wounds

IT's NEARING THE END of June and the hospital's budget worries have abated. At the last minute the state has come up with the promised cash. Within weeks, of course, Dr. Steinhauer and his team will be thrown into yet another round of negotiations for the next year's cash. The great unresolved question of who pays for those who cannot pay for themselves goes on. Dr. Steinhauer, when asked about this, was philosophical.

"Every generation," he said, "believes in finding a permanent solution, but there never is one."

And so his administration exists, as all previous Med administrations have existed, in a kind of perpetual limbo, a strange twilight world of management reports, consultants and internal audits, secure only in the oft-repeated mantra that "they can't afford to close us down. Where would all these people go?" Invariably in making this remark the speaker will wave one arm around to indicate the poor "self-pay" patients sitting on the steps across the road from the administration building.

The implication, of course, is that there are vested interests in keeping the Med there—but keeping it poor. The suggestion is that the Med's existence means that private hospitals can profitably exist without the aggravation of caring for those who cannot pay.

This is a curious security, though, and cannot, surely, be good for staff morale and motivation. The nurses, Dr. Steinhauer has already told me, are human—they're not angels. They stay at the Med because the rates of pay—though not the patients—are competitive.

"My impression," says Steinhauer, by way of answer, "is that the staff have become immune to the 'crisis.' If a crisis is permanent it cannot, by definition, be a crisis. So there is a general assumption that 'Steinhauer will find something, somewhere.' What really exercises the minds of the nurses is what they experience day to day. So they want to know that there are enough nurses. Many see it as a recruitment problem, which is not about money but about supply."

My conversations with the nurses have revealed a second motivation—there is pride in the work people do, both that it is so challenging and, often, that it bears some resemblance to the caring profession they believe in. "At private hospitals," one nurse told me, "things are very different. There it matters whether the phone rings twice before you answer it. Here there is a different agenda. Here they want people to get better."

"What they worry about," says Steinhauer, "is the gaps they experience where they work. It's not about supplies or money or about how big or small my deficit is. What nurses want is enough nurses for the patient load they see in front of them.

"Of course," he adds, "this means money, but nurses don't think about it as money. Which is a problem for a fixed-income hospital like this."

By June, Steinhauer has found "something, somewhere" and the nurses can relax—although "relax" is probably the wrong word, especially for the nurses in the trauma center.

"You should be here for July Fourth," they have repeated. "That's when it gets real busy."

ON THIS PARTICULAR DAY in June the trauma unit is air-conditioned and cool, but outside the temperature and the humidity have climbed into the nineties. It will, the forecasters say, be like that for some days to come. I move back into the now familiar corridors of the trauma center. By now I am familiar to most people there. People no longer stop to read the small print on the badge the Med has given me, the one that lets me wander freely through doors marked "Authorized Personnel Only." People no longer ask if I need help, perhaps because I no longer look lost. The security staff wave me through. "You still here?" they ask from time to time. "How's it going?"

I've only just met Carol Woods, CRNA, but we are getting on well. She's concealed by her OR gown but she has a friendly face and she seems happy enough to talk to me. We cover what I have come to think of as "the basics" in double-quick time: forty-one years old, three kids, in the process of a messy divorce. "Finally," she says with a tired smile. Carol comes from Philadelphia, graduated in Connecticut and has been working as a nurse since 1980—"back when we had to wear white uniforms and would give up our seats if a doctor walked into the room. It's unimaginable now."

I ask her the question I have been wanting to ask every nurse: So have you ever saved someone's life? What does it feel like?

Carol takes this question very seriously indeed. She nods slowly.

"I have," she says, "I have. There have been times when I made the difference between life and death. Not long ago there was a patient who had a tracheotomy tube. He was in an MVA or something. And he pulled the tube out, couldn't breathe and went into full arrest. So anyway, I got it back in and you could hear him come back to life. Suddenly he's getting air and the machines are beeping again."

She pauses to search my face, to check that I understand.

"It was a pretty good feeling," she says, "to know that I was the one that made the difference."

IT DOESN'T ALWAYS work out that way. Sometimes people get things wrong, and sometimes people die anyway. Sometimes patients, crazed with pain, rip out their tracheotomy tubes, and no one is able to get them back in in time. Sometimes they're wrongly inserted or inserted too late. And sometimes the Med receives patients who are dead or so near to dead it makes no difference. "For other hospitals, 'critical' is nearly dead. For us, it's manageable," I was told on my first visit to the Med. Such confidence and pride is admirable. But the human body is finite. It can take only so much, and sometimes people die.

✚

IT'S A HOT SUMMER afternoon and nothing seems unusual in the corridors of the Med. Residents are snapping off their gloves. Nurses are going back to their stations. A couple of paramedics leave by the special door to the ambulance parking lot and I feel the heat from outside as the doors close behind them. A police officer walks by with a clipboard.

"What happened to him?" I ask a nurse, indicating a man on a stretcher. He looks like any other patient waiting to be taken for a CT scan or an X-ray.

"Shooting," he says. "Chest wound."

Seeing the look on my face, he confirms what I had begun to suspect.

"He didn't make it. You missed the action."

I MAY HAVE "missed the action," but I can imagine it. There is a pattern to these things. We can all bring to mind the speeded-up film. We've seen too many movies not to. I can imagine the team of nurses and physicians bent over the dying man. I can imagine the beeping machines and the shouts of "Clear!" followed by the *whump* of the respirator pads being applied, the sound that they exaggerate on TV.

Now, in what should be the silence of a death, the corridor is busy. People come in, some hurrying, some talking. Comments fill the air:

"Only in America."

"I hear it's a real funny movie."

"The most violent and aggressive country in the world."

"We know the relatives?"

"Terrible. I shot nine on the sixteenth."

"What are you doing for lunch?"

And then just as quickly everybody has gone somewhere else. The corridor, momentarily, is empty except for me and the covered body of a dead man, who, I have learned, was only in Memphis for the day. He died from a single gunshot wound to the chest after a drive-by shooting only a couple of miles from the Med.

In the silence I find myself looking intently not at the body of the dead man but at the triage room where the nurses and physicians tried to save his life. There is the usual mess. Tissues and paper and the wrappings from bandages and syringes litter the floor. The OR bed is covered in bloodied sheets. Over in a corner there is a fragment of cloth. It looks like part of someone's denim shirt.

My eyes move slowly up the wall to where a chart hangs describing the insignia of various gangs whose members are regular patients in the shock trauma unit at the Med. Earlier, Kerry Lyons showed them to me and told me about the various gangs—the Gangster Disciples, the New Breed Black Gangsters, the Latin Kings, the Cobra Stones. When she was working in Chicago the nurses would go on a "gang refresher" course each year. One time she and some colleagues were held at gunpoint by gang members who wanted the body of one of their "members" back "for some kind of ritual."

"What did you do?"

"I said, 'Help yourself!'" She laughed, and I had no way of

knowing whether this was for real, although many nurses have told me how both in policy and in practice they will not try to stop anyone with a gun.

"The gangs are less of a thing in Memphis," Kerry told me. "These are franchises of the other places—Chicago, LA. It's a business thing. The local branch manager takes a cut but the real money goes to some big shot someplace else. That's always been the story for Memphis. But still, they are a problem and we have to be aware."

Less of "a thing" is still a thing, and later that day I found myself looking a little more closely at a group of young men hanging around on the stairs outside the trauma center, looking for any of the telltale insignia that they carry, like so many red badges of courage.

IN THE SUDDEN SILENCE of the hallway outside the triage room I am aware only of the infinite melancholy of the death of this anonymous man who was in Memphis for only a day but who drove down the wrong street at the wrong time and died in a pool of blood, his underwear cut from him and lying bloodied and forgotten on the floor.

The electronic doors down the passage swish open and one of the cleaners comes past, pushing a trolley of cleaning materials. She doesn't glance at the covered body but heads straight into the triage room to clean up the mess. She, like all the nurses, is wearing surgical gloves and a mask. Her movements have a kind of slow, operatic grace. Perhaps it is that she carries herself with the stately pace of a diva in mid-aria. Perhaps it is just the practiced, disinterested air with which she swoops to clear the floor or sprays the beds with disinfectant. Or perhaps it is just that I can see her eyes passing thoughtlessly over the very details that I find so telling: the "sharps" disposal box filled almost to overflowing, the discarded newspaper brought in with the dying man and the generations of yellow iodine stains on the floor.

What, I wonder, is she thinking as she scoops up the remnants of the man's shirt and his discarded sneakers, one strangely new and white, the other dark with congealing blood?

How much time has passed? It feels like an hour, but perhaps it was just minutes.

Oblivious to me and my thoughts, the cleaner rebags the bins—red for hazardous materials, blue for scrubs, black for "ordinary crap." And then she, too, is gone and I am alone in the corridor.

And somewhere not too far away a siren sounds.

THE REST, HAMLET SAID as he departed for his coveted oblivion, is silence.

For the nurses of the Med "the rest" is more of the same. As quickly as the silence filled the hall, the sounds of people, trolleys, walkie-talkies and the restless doors fill this little space again.

As if by magic—although of course it is triggered by the message from Medcom—the hall fills with nurses and physicians. Then Carol, the CRNA, comes through from her little office in Trauma OR. Joel Gingery, RN, is getting an IV drip ready.

The ambulance arrives. It brings a teenage boy "ped-struck" in Whitehaven. He has been IDed by the EMT people at the scene, but Kerry can't get ahold of his parents. Apparently, they've gone to Texas for the weekend. Someone has a number for someone who might know.

"Are we sure?" Kerry yells. "I don't want to call the wrong person."

"We're sure."

"I hate this stuff," Kerry says as she dials. "He's just a kid."

The man beneath the sheet in the next room was a kid, too, not so very long ago. I can't help looking at him again, temporarily forgotten because, on good days at least, life goes on. The kid from Whitehaven is not going to die anytime soon.

CHAPTER 22

Money Matters

"THAT'S THE STORY," says Rhonda Nelson, RN. "That's my year."

I look at the 500-odd pages of computer printouts she has just handed me, all characteristically bound in Med-blue binding. The title on the cover: REGIONAL MEDICAL CENTER AT MEMPHIS. MONTHLY FINANCE PACKAGE. MAY 31. It's mid-June and the figures for the previous month are just out. Rhonda's year is drawing to an end. The Med has not—yet—closed down, in part or as a whole. But it might.

Losses for the year to date total $11 million.

"An unfavorable variance?" I say, by way of an icebreaker.

"Compared to budget?" Rhonda laughs. "I think we can say it's unfavorable—by about eleven million. We didn't plan to make a loss!"

The document has a helpful executive summary and I run my eyes over it while Rhonda checks through her e-mails.

Rhonda Nelson

May was, by the standards of Med finances, a good month. The average daily census was 296 patients, 3 percent up on budget. The departments experiencing the greatest increases in in-patient days are the ones I am familiar with: Trauma, Labor and Delivery, the Newborn Center.

As a result, gross patient revenue was up by $3.7 million, and by month's end the hospital had 16.7 days' cash on hand, up from 10.4 the previous month. The doom and gloom has, temporarily, abated.

"Quite a year," I say.

"Well, I've had easier. But we're coming out of it better than I thought." Rhonda is dressed in her regulation-issue navy suit. Her hair and makeup are as before, neat, professional. Nothing is out of place.

When she talks about her year she gets a curious expression, calculating what my agenda is, where my interests really lie.

I could tell her, but it is typical of Rhonda that she doesn't ask outright. It's more her style to work things through on her own, to hedge her bets and then wait and see. We talk about the year a bit, the highs and lows, and I ask what stands out in her memory. Her answer surprises me—but perhaps it should not have.

"Well, we had the union business."

On and off I have heard snippets about the "union business," but during the time I was at the hospital it was not dormant exactly, but not at the top of the agenda either. And it was not something people liked to talk about—or not to me. Several months before I came to the Med there was a dispute in the trauma unit. Someone lost their job and other nurses were not happy about this. There was talk of a union. Someone got in touch with the Service Employees International Union, and Local 205 in Nashville sent some organizers to Memphis. They started leafleting the nurses in the parking garage, talking about grievances, collecting signatures. They started calling people at home.

"It happens every few years," Dr. Steinhauer told me the day before. "And we, the board, thought about it for a while. As a public hospital we are not under the NLRB [National Labor Relations Board], so we don't have to recognize or work with any union. So after a while the board just said no. This is not how we do things in Tennessee. No union. And that was that."

"Really?" I asked, not believing things are ever that simple. After all, Memphis is the place where Dr. Martin Luther King came to address a rally of sanitation workers and was murdered. The workers were striking for union recognition and for higher wages, although, as was widely acknowledged at the time, the real issue was not wages but dignity. "I Am a Man," read the placards, and when Martin Luther King spoke on the day before he was assassinated, he put it like this: "You are demanding that this city will respect the dignity of labor. So often we overlook the work and the significance of those who are not in professional jobs, of those who are not in the so-called big jobs. But let me say to you tonight that whenever you are engaged in work that serves humanity and is for the building of humanity, it has dignity and it has worth."

"It'll come round again," said Dr. Steinhauer with a smile. "Probably after I'm gone."

"Oh, maybe five to eight years," says Rhonda. "Thing was, there were some people who were disgruntled and it forced us to look at things."

I am aware that this is the conciliatory Rhonda speaking. This is the voice of the victor, but in truth the battle does not appear to have been very bitter or very hard fought.

The organizers were pretty aggressive, several nurses told me—and it is revealing that on this subject alone, none wanted to be on the record. And they—or the issue—did force management to buy the loyalty of the staff.

"I represent myself" was a typical response when I asked what people thought of the union.

"I was in a union once," said another, "and it don't make no difference. We're all going to get paid the same anyway."

"If I was just getting basic," said a third, "I would have signed up. The money I'm getting means I don't need to."

"We're pennies ahead of other hospitals around here," says Rhonda, "in terms of rates. We're just ahead. Our nurses have had two pay raises this year. The other thing we had to look at was staffing levels. Were we expecting people to do too much and so on. It was difficult because it was during a time of rapid turnover and so on, but what we did was we got some recruiting experts in and they looked at the whole thing and shored up the whole wages-and-benefits package. So we know that no other hospital in the city pays better than us."

Steinhauer told me a similar story.

"We have maintained parity in this market," he said. "Our nurses do okay. But the other thing we wanted to make people understand is that we can't have a very rigid labor market here. We're demand-driven. Levels fluctuate."

This is, of course, the hard edge of the welcoming and open management I have come to take for granted at the Med.

"So have you bought the nurses off?" I asked Dr. Steinhauer.

I got a trademark smile in response.

"The work here is hard," he said, "in part because we have so few stereotypical patients. In another hospital you might find yourself doing the same procedure five times a week. But not here. Here we have to expect the unexpected, and so the workload is heavy. Now, in any group of nurses you're going to find two classes of nurses. There are those who will stick through thick and thin. And there are those who—how shall I put this?—are more vulnerable to being sick on the day before a public holiday.

"Idealism is one thing. And many of our nurses are idealists. Like me, they believe in what they're doing. But you can't staff a hospital on the basis of idealism. There aren't that many to go around! So the big change this year is that the nurses are dramatically better paid than they were. And there's nothing we can do about that. We have no choice."

Dr. Steinhauer put on a sardonic smile.

"When Baptist put up their rates by two dollars per hour it took Methodist all of six days to match it. What else could we do?"

The union thing was, mostly, about money. But the management nevertheless fought it on a range of issues. The communications department gave me a series of leaflets handed out during the "difficult period," and it is possible to deduce the story from that.

Volume 1, Issue 1, of "Know the Facts" (subtitled "The Truths Healthcare Professionals Really Need to Know about the SEIU Local 205") devotes a whole page to just nine words: "Union Dues go Toward Supporting the Union, Not You!" Volume 2 is similarly encouraging. "A Strike Can be Costly not only to your Pocketbook, but also Your Career." And so on. The management at the Med are not the first—and surely not the last—to try to persuade workers that anyone joining a union would be "giving away your individual rights to the union."

By May both nurses and management were telling me that "the union thing" had "gone away," although I suspect that Dr. Steinhauer's assessment came closer. "They'll be back." And indeed on June 7 the Memphis Commercial Appeal reported that "as part of its drive to unionize registered nurses, the Service Employees International Union (SEIU) plans a rally and prayer vigil today outside the Regional Medical Center at Memphis.

The union, which represents more than 770,000 health workers, is pushing the hospital board to recognize it as the representative of 500 RNs who work at the publicly-funded hospital."

The hospital's response was to reiterate that it had no plans to recognize the union.

"We believe union representation could interfere with our ability to provide continuous patient care, particularly given our current financial situation," Gloria Thomas, vice president of human resources, is reported as saying.

Well, she would say that, wouldn't she? And the union will say what unions say. Although union activity is reasonably strong in Memphis—FedEx, for example, is the city's largest employer and its pilots and drivers are organized through the Teamsters and other unions—this is not true of the health sector.

Rhonda, whose budget pays for all the nurses, has a slightly different spin. "We pay the nurses well, and to make that work we had to spend a long time looking at the high-dollar impact areas—which means older nurses and agency nurses. Because agency nurses are expensive. We're now much better staffed than we were and so we have been able to cut down on agency nurses."

"But not on older nurses," I say, thinking of several I have met.

"Older nurses are worth it," says Rhonda flatly. "There's no substitute for experience."

Chapter 23

American as Apple Pie

THE MUZZLE VELOCITY of a standard police-issue Smith & Wesson .38 revolver is something like 750 feet per second. A bullet leaving the gun at that speed and hitting human flesh will leave a whole lot of damage. It depends on the bullet, of course. It is not just the torn flesh and ruptured arteries, not just the trail of shattered bone and sinew that the bullet leaves behind. It can also be that the bullet itself breaks up and scatters.

It can be that this is what was intended.

SINCE I FIRST STARTED visiting the Med, the nurses have told me to be there on July Fourth weekend. "Nothing of importance happened today," George III famously wrote in his diary on July 4, 1776. Perhaps he would have said the same in the Med. "It won't be different," I was told.

"But it gets real busy," they said. "It's our busiest time of year. You really want to be here then."

By "real busy," of course, they mean the trauma wards. They mean that in the heat of summer, in the main holiday celebrating national independence, in the festival of being American, more people will assert their right to cause themselves or others to be "bent, broke or bleeding." They will do this with cars and firearms, with knives and lead pipes and anything else they can get their hands on. And one by one they will be brought to the Med to be repaired—if possible.

So it is that I find myself in the Med in the buildup to July Fourth. I am spending most of my time—feeling pretty ghoulish—in Trauma, which I have come to think of as the cutting edge of nursing, watching the cases come in, trying to get a feel again for the human stories behind the statistics that will, in time, emerge in one of the many internal reports that the Med generates about itself.

Many of the nurses I now know well are there. In Shock Trauma, Teddy Winney is holding court on the subject of his forthcoming fishing weekend. Kerry Lyons is doing what she does, looking for a bed for the man in bay 8. This is slightly problematic because the man in bay 8 is almost seven feet tall and weighs well over 300 pounds. Joel Gingery is there, too, and Shannon Glenn.

Over in Trauma OR, I find Lynn Regester.

"Come on in," says Lynn. "Have something to eat."

It's a curious moment. In the windowless room in the bowels of Trauma OR where the nurses relax and eat and watch TV there is a feast laid on for July Fourth. But hospital rhythms are not the rhythms of the outside world, and so I find myself faced with a mountain of barbecued ribs and potato salad at only 10:15 in the morning.

"You gotta eat," says Lynn. "We don't know how long this thing's going to take."

"This thing" is the partial reconstruction of a twenty-three-year-old woman's face. It is an intricate and complicated piece of surgery and everybody knows that no matter how perfectly it is done, she will still be scarred for the rest of her life. She may or may not—the consensus goes—be lucky to be alive.

But for the moment the discussion is about the food and Frank's plans to harvest a stand of pines growing on his land. Frank Williams, CRNA, and his wife are both nurses; but once he qualified as a CRNA it was no longer necessary for her to work. Now she devotes herself to raising their two sons and working on the farm they have bought 105 miles away in northern Arkansas. "Mostly beef," he says. "We have about two hundred and forty acres."

As a CRNA working forty-eight hours a week (two twenty-four-hour shifts), Frank stands to be making over $100,000 a year.

"So which earns you more?" I ask.

"Oh, this," he replies. "Compared to this, farming is just a hobby. It's like golf, something I do for fun. This is what makes farming possible."

This is a far cry from the idea of nursing I had when I first started visiting the Med, and a far cry, I am sure, from the general image of nursing. I am not sure which part I find most surprising—the rates, or the idea of a 200-mile commute to work.

Dr. Steinhauer points to the marketplace. Demand outstrips supply and so prices have risen. Fast. They look set to continue to rise, because even though supply will increase—especially with more men entering the profession—there is no sign that it will increase as fast as the demand.

And it's hurting. A *New York Times Magazine* article in March 2003 reported that the nursing shortage accounts for 31 percent more postsurgery deaths in some hospitals. Rather astutely the article's author, Sara Corbett, notes that "if profit-driven health care, which brought about nationwide layoffs of nurses in the early '90s, is largely to blame for the current shortage, the public's perception of nurses as beneficent and mild may be helping to sustain it." The long-standing—and nowadays wholly inaccurate—classification of nurses as "saints and sex objects" still persists. Part of the problem, Barbara Blakeney of the American Nurses Association is quoted as saying, is that people do not know exactly what it is that nurses do. "Nurses prevent bad things from happening," she said. "And it is much more difficult to measure what does happen as opposed to what doesn't."

In the Med this is no longer a sustainable view. Nurses are active, necessary and—at least in market terms—valued.

But a nurse earning enough to subsidize a 200-acre beef farm? Enough to raise two sons in a good life? This really is something. Of course, it is the anesthesiology that makes the money and that means Frank can do this. As an "ordinary" registered nurse he would be earning half that amount.

But still.

A gentleman farmer subsidizing his hobby through nursing?

Crisis, I find myself asking, what crisis?

✚

IT'S THAT QUIET time again in Trauma OR, a feeling I have become used to. The nurses' room empties as people finish eating and move off.

While Lynn and the others go to join the group of people waiting in Shock Trauma, I read through the notice of today's operation.

"D & I. GSW & Reconstruction," it reads.

"D & I" means "debridement and irrigation," which we would call "cleaning the wound," although in fact it means a little more than that. Debridement is the process of removing all dead tissue—a great source of infection—before surgery begins. "Irrigation" is self-explanatory, as is the now so familiar "GSW."

There are various sources of statistics for the incidence of gunshot wounds in Memphis. Perhaps the Med's are as revealing as any: 12 percent of the 4,000-plus patients admitted to Trauma at the Med each year have been shot, or have shot themselves. That's something like 500 patients, ten every week. Two every day. To a single hospital in a midsized metropolitan area in the mid-South. For those of us who come from less gun-saturated environments this is a very difficult number to comprehend. The United Kingdom—despite alarming rises in recent years—has something like 800 homicides a year, of which perhaps 8 percent are by firearms. So sixty-five firearm homicides a year in a country of 60 million people. Memphis—let's include the city, and Shelby County and the surrounding metropolitan areas—has a population of 1.5 million people. And each year there are something like 200 homicides.

Fifty percent of which are by gunshot.

Similarly, the number of suicide attempts far exceeds those in the U.K.

More than 50 percent of suicide attempts involve firearms.

"You get used to it," says Lynn, meaning the idea rather than the feeling. "People shoot each other a lot. They all have guns, that's the problem."

LYNN'S GLAD TO BE working today. Her husband has invited a couple of people around for a cookout, which is not really her thing. "I don't like being bitten by mosquitoes. I guess I'm just not a big outdoorsy kind of person. So I pass on all that. But he likes it," she says, "so he can do it. I'm happy to be here, doing my job.

"We should go. No sense in hanging around. That's the thing about this job. You can make it hard for yourself or you can make it easy for yourself. But the fact is that what you don't do now, you're going to have to do later," she says.

I follow Lynn and we "cover up" (which is to say, put on masks and head and shoe covers) and go into the OR.

"First I need to check that everything is ready. Then we can go get the patient."

I WATCH IN SILENCE as Lynn does her own preparation of the OR. The supply people have been in, the cleaners, too. And they have left everything shipshape. But Lynn has her own experience to draw on.

"I'm thinking about the operation," she says, in answer to

my question. "I'm guessing what the surgeon will need. I play it like a movie. What's going to happen? What will he need? What might go wrong?"

"Nurses prevent bad things from happening," *The New York Times* reported.

I must have raised an eyebrow at this point—or perhaps it is just that she knows journalists are far more interested in "when things go wrong" than when they go "right."

"Well, it could be anything," she notes dryly. "A case like this, the most important thing is you don't want to lose the airways. You have got to keep them patent. Or maybe they will have severed an artery. Something like that. The thing about an operation is, it is a life-and-death thing. And on a case like this the most likely complication is that the patient might die, because she's pretty messed up."

She sighs and stops for a moment—and I'm glad of that, too. Lynn seems to me to have lost none of her humanity in the many hard years she has spent in the operating theater.

"Does it happen often?" I ask. "People dying in the OR."

"Not really," she says. "Not really. I think in my career maybe two people have actually died in the OR. 'Cause, like I say, if they look like they are dying, they close 'em up and get them out of there pretty fast."

She goes back to checking her lists. "So anyway," she says, "I like to check everything beforehand. I'll be circulating on this one and the more I do now, the less running I might have to do later. But I know they're gonna have me run for something. You always do."

She finishes up. "Let's go see what's happening," she says.

✛

THE FACIAL RECONSTRUCTION is scheduled for 11 A.M., but as we move out of the OR a call comes in. There's a trauma patient coming by air, five minutes.

"We gotta wait and see what it is first, see whether the surgeons are needed. Because once they're operating there is no way anybody gets out until it is finished."

"Unknown 850," says the card at the nurses' station. "Female, 24. TICU Bay 19. Duration 6 hours" (except Lynn laughs and says it should be eight hours. "Always," she says. "Every time they estimate less than it actually takes. I don't know why they do that. They showing off or something?"). Then there's a list of the required supplies, one Lynn has already checked off in the OR. She goes through it again, just to be sure—or to cut down on the running.

Lynn has a steady quality to her. She doesn't move fast, but she moves with purpose. She's not one to get overexcited. I watch her in the small throng of nurses and residents, anesthetists, radiologists, security people and the hospital chaplain gathering at the door. Others are chatting, making jokes, acting out a little. Lynn is completely contained. If it comes, it comes, she seems to be thinking. If I'm needed, I'm needed.

I GO BACK TO THE OR and look again at the patient's card. I know a little about her, this unknown woman of twenty-four. Her wounds are sufficiently dramatic for people to have remarked on it—and yet it is an everyday story at the Med. On my first visit, on a freezing January day, I had not been in the hospital fifteen minutes when we heard the wail of ambulance sirens. That time it was two people, both with gunshot wounds. Both died. "He" had shot his "girlfriend" in a lover's rage and then—mortified, one assumes—turned his gun on himself. Both lived long enough to get to the Med. Both died soon after.

Both were teenagers.

Today's patient has also been shot, apparently by her jealous lover—or would-be lover—who then shot himself. But he died, and she has survived. His weapon of choice was, according to police, a sawed-off shotgun, and he fired a single blast into her face. "The worst shotgun wounds are those at close range because that's when the pellet energy is highest," I was told. The pellets in this case ripped into the woman's face and cheek and jaw, stripping the flesh and shattering bone and gristle. Her nose and eyes are intact and seemingly undamaged, but her lower face is a flapping mess of skin and flesh. It is not clear to me how the surgeons can ever hope to put something like that back together.

"You'll be amazed," says Lynn, "at what we can do."

For some reason I find myself inordinately pleased that she said "we," that without thinking she has included herself in the definition of who it is that puts people like this back "together." I have no doubt, also, that I will be amazed.

"Mind you, you'll be amazed at what people can do to each other."

Sadly, this no longer surprises me.

✚

LYNN COMES BACK from Shock Trauma. The incoming patient was "no big deal." It's time for the operation to begin.

I walk the corridors with her and Frank to bay 19 in TICU,
where they "collect" the patient and wheel her through to the
operating room.

An orderly comes with them to the OR. "She's a big one,
Miss Lynn," he says. "I don't want you to go hurting your back."

The patient at this point is covered in bandages. They move
her over to the OR bed without too much trouble.

"You should put your mask on now," she says. "I'm going to
start opening some things."

Cheryl joins her. I take up a perch on a stool and settle in. It's
going to be a long one.

CHAPTER 24

Slow Train Coming

I SPENT NEARLY twenty-four hours in that operating room over the next day and a half, first with Lynn as the surgeons slowly, steadily started to pull together the patient's tattered and torn face. From time to time they invite me in closer to "take a look." The flaps of brown skin hang loosely. There is no blood, only a kind of redness to the flesh. Once everything has been cleaned, with the patient so heavily sedated it really does just look like—well, meat. The patient is a large woman.

Gradually, as the hours pass, something resembling a face—a bruised and battered face, to be sure, but nonetheless a face—takes shape. The hole that was there is reclaimed piecemeal—a fragment of bone here, a piece of plate there, a slither of skin here. Her eyes are intact, shielded and closed for the operation, and half her nose is there. I realize that what's really missing, the quintessentially human attribute, are her lips—lips for talking and kissing, for tasting and smiling.

Sometimes in the hours that pass, there is music on. From time to time it goes off, or perhaps I just don't notice it. The surgeons have a collegiate relationship with Becky and Lynn. They talk easily and the slow medical processes happen within a cocoon of conversation.

"It's getting hot in here."

"Sure is a hot one."

"Man, this is sad."

"He shot himself, you say?"

"Shot her and then himself."

"Man, he got that the wrong way round."

"Merciful father!"

"So what are we gonna do?"

"D and I."

"We're gonna do the best we can."

Time becomes unimportant in the OR. There is a clock on the wall, and from time to time Lynn, in her role as circulating nurse, makes notes on the various forms, and each time she records the time. But this is a record of time that will matter later. For the time being time is not the issue, just as speed is not the issue. Everybody in the room is on a twenty-four-hour shift. This can take all day and it won't matter. It can take all night, too.

The important thing is to get it right.

To do the best they can.

✚

"I can't think of a better way to spend my day," says one surgeon.

The music is on loud now. The radio is positioned between the two operating rooms and the speakers echo between them.

I notice that in her charts Lynn has noted the pre-op diagnosis. "GSW to Face," she writes. She sees me looking at the space for post-op diagnosis.

"It'll be the same," she says, with a weary smile. "That diagnosis ain't never gonna change!"

They're in the groove now. "Let the reconstruction begin," says Lynn.

"Cheryl, how old are you?" asks a resident.

"Forty-five."

"I was going to say twenty-five."

"Give this man whatever he wants," Cheryl says to Lynn. She's pretending not to be pleased.

The patient came into the OR at 12:55. The D & I started at 13:45. The first incision was made at 14:30; at roughly the same moment an unfortunate ad for a supermarket chain comes on the radio. ". . . the best cuts of meat for your holiday." I'm pretty sure I'm the only one who notices.

"How much will all this cost?" I ask, inappropriately.

"Her?" says Lynn. "Hundreds of thousands. Because it's not

just the operation. She's going to be here a long time, a month or more. She'll need a trach [tracheotomy]. Probably she'll get some kind of infection, because she's got this whole shattered jaw thing."

The thing about an operation is there is plenty of time to talk. Someone has turned down the radio and Lynn starts telling me the full story of how she got into nursing.

"I always wanted to do nursing. Even as a kid. This was 'round the time desegregation started—you know, things were becoming possible that weren't possible before. But even so, we had a lot of racist counselors. In that sense when I left school— this was in the sixties—things hadn't changed. The counselor at my school said nursing wasn't an option for me. It was 'secretary or housekeeping,' that's what she said. So I had to go to business school and learned to type and all that. And pretty soon I became a court stenographer and I wanted to go and work in court."

Lynn looks at me. In full scrubs and mask it is hard to tell what she is thinking. She doesn't seem angry but there is an even telling to the story that gives me pause.

"But I couldn't get a place because it was like all the jobs were held by old white ladies who hadn't died yet. So I went to work as a secretary in a bank and I did that for a year. But none of this was what I wanted to do?"

Lynn makes it a question to make sure I am keeping up. I am, but in the back of my mind I am marveling at her determination to qualify for a job that back then—this was the early seventies—was paying little more than minimum wage.

"So I went back to college and started taking more credits,

hoping that eventually they would admit me to a nursing program. And eventually they did. But still I didn't qualify as a nurse; I was just an OR technician. And I did that for fifteen years."

Fifteen years. The OR is not the only place that time seems to slip by faster than is reasonable.

"But what I really wanted to do was work in the OR as a nurse. And I talked to nurses about it and there was one—she was a white nurse, an older white nurse—she was the one that said, 'Go back to school. If that's what you want to do, you must do it.' So I did. I went back to school and I got my RN."

"And you qualified . . . when?"

"Nineteen ninety-one. I got my license in 1991. But that was still with only an associate degree. I had to go back to school again to do my bachelor's degree. I finally did that this year."

I am slightly in awe of this tale of a thirty-year quest to fulfill what on the surface seems like a modest dream: to be a nurse.

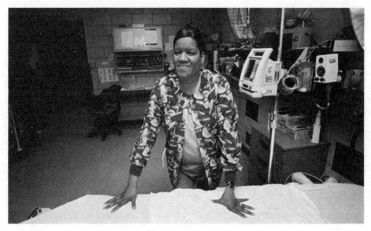

Lynn Regester

And I am dimly aware that for this dream to have held through the many slights, setbacks and disappointments that must have littered Lynn's working life, it must have been built on something pretty solid. And of course it was. Dig a little deeper with Lynn and you can hear the anger and disappointment. She is no radical, not one to scream and shout. But she knows and feels it strongly that life has asked more of her than of many. And she has answered in full measure.

"People are quick to play the race card," she says. "Black and white. You get white people telling you about some part of town, some bad part of town. They tell you they never go there and then they tell you what it's like. How can they know?

"And you get black folk telling you how bad it is, going on the radio and talking and everything. Now, it's true. We have a history and we black people got off to a poor start. But that's not what I think now. What I say is this: You should do what you want to do. Don't make it about race or about haves and have-nots. This is 2003. This is about choice."

Choices, nevertheless, that Lynn feels sometimes come too easily. She found the process of doing her bachelor's degree at Union University a dispiriting one.

"I sometimes think that for some it's too easy now," she says. "When I first went to school, if you failed, you failed. But now these kids negotiate. If they didn't get the grade they go and talk to their professor about it. See if they can push it up a little. It means that for me school here was a breeze. My sister teaches at a university in North Carolina and she says it is the same there. The students are consumers and in this country the consumer is king."

I cannot help glancing at the patient on the table, neither a consumer—since her insurance status is unknown—nor a king.

"I worry about our tomorrows," she says. "What will we do when people have forgotten how to work?"

She turns to complete some notes. Surgery—which started at 13:45—finishes at 20:25. The patient leaves the OR at 20:35.

"She'll be back for more surgery," says Lynn. "Else how's she gonna eat?"

CHAPTER 25

Saying Good-bye

UNKNOWN PATIENT 850 was back in the OR the following morning. Not for any complications, but to have a G-tube (gastrointestinal feeding tube) inserted.

"I don't know why they didn't just do it yesterday," says Becky Laster, RN. "They already had her on the table and all. I guess this means they think she'll live."

It takes me a moment or two to work out what Becky is saying. Why bother with the expense of a G-tube or tracheotomy if the patient is not going to live? These are, in one sense, routine medical choices, and in another sense a challenge to our value system. Dr. Korones in the Newborn Center's voice rose when he described to me his outrage at reading papers in which doctors—doctors!—have calculated whether it is "worth" trying to save 1,000-gram or 750-gram babies. "How can they say that?" he asked rhetorically. "Aren't they doctors?" The smallest baby that survived at the Med had a birth weight, he thinks, of just under 400 grams. Other doctors have told me the same.

It is a familiar litany of complaint, the iniquity of having to think about money when someone's health is at stake. One doctor described for me in some detail how he might try to buck the system; how, for example, he will admit a patient who doesn't really need to be admitted because that way the $2,000 bill will be covered by Tenncare, whereas if he is not admitted he won't be able to pay the $300 his treatment really costs.

SHARON LUCUS IS the CRNA for this op. Becky is circulating and Hester Moore, RN, is scrub nurse.

"It's a simple one," says Sharon. "How hard can it be?"

"Don't say that," says Becky. "Nothing's ever simple."

But this time it is, and the chart reflects that. For once they are "out of there" in less time than that predicted by the surgeons. "OR entry: 10:35," reads the form. "Surgery starts: 10:55. Ends 11:55."

The patient has been taken back to the intensive care unit and I hang around in the OR with Becky. A moment before we watched as the bandages and covers were taken off much of the patient's face. There is a kind of peace that comes with survival. For all that her skin is bruised and puffy, for all that her mouth has been replaced by a jagged outcrop of skin and stitching and for all that there is a tube sticking out of her chest, like a knife handle, the patient is sleeping and breathing quietly.

"Trouble is," says Becky, "I know her mother. She comes from the same part of town I grew up in."

Perhaps, I reflect, when this patient recovers sufficiently to be taken out of sedation, she will get to know the nurses. Per-

haps, like my landlord, Dennis, she will find them rude and in-
hospitable. Perhaps they, too, will pull "her dang tubes out."

Perhaps one day she will describe the nurses at the Med in
less than flattering terms.

But I doubt it. Watching her as she is wheeled back to her
room on Trauma Intensive Care Unit, I am pretty sure that one
day she will say, "Those nurses saved my life." She will say it
without thinking about it and she will say it because it will
be true.

In the time I spent in the Med, I came across various nurses
who have been "in"—or had relatives "in"—as patients. Always these stories have been told to me in the context of praise
for the standard of service the Med provides and usually to dis-
prove the notion that a hospital providing for poor patients provides poor care. But I have become aware that there is a second
part to this transition from nurse to patient, and a much more
complicated one. Barbara, at Hospital Wing, told me about her
brother who died while she was on another flight. "I knew they
had gone to pick up someone in an MVA. But I didn't know it
was him." She was on another call at the time. "It really
brought it home, you know. We care about these patients, but
we keep them as patients. We don't make them family. Which
makes it real hard when they are family."

It is hardest in Trauma. As Teddy once put it to me, "No one
comes through those doors because they got lucky." Or as Hester told me after the operation on Unknown Patient 850:
"Ninety-nine percent of what I do has to be done because of

someone else's stupidity. That's my job security—other people being stupid." I think of Peggy in Burn: "We're seeing people at their worst." And I think of Marye in the HIV clinic, whose relentless optimism with her patients works until but not during the moment she tells them they are not going to get disability, at least not under her signature. And I think of my landlord Dennis and his arm, which lay on the table, "just lay there," while the doctors and nurses at the Med tried seven times to sew it back on.

On this particular summer morning in OR Becky has a little free time. "They've got another trach [tracheotomy]," she says, "but they can't find the family to get permission to do the operation. So we get to sit and wait a little. We get to have some food."

In the nurses' room there are the leftovers from the July Fourth feast. I start talking a little about the operation I witnessed on the unknown patient, whose face was blown away with the pellets from her boyfriend's shotgun. It turns out Becky recognized her.

"I know her mother," Becky says again. "I probably know a whole bunch of people she knows. He sure messed her up good."

She's lucky to be alive, I suggest.

"Well, I don't know about that," says Becky. "If that's what she wants, *then* she's lucky. But we'll only know if it's what she wants when she wakes up."

"And even then she won't be sure," says Hester.

"Luck isn't always what you think. Ain't that what people say? Be careful what you wish for."

But you saved her life?

"We did. Us. The surgeons. The Med. The whole system

worked. She got shot in the mouth and should have died. But she didn't because everything was there. The ambulance that brought her. The EMTs. The fire department. Us too. We did what we had to and it didn't cost her a cent. It wasn't about the money. Everything worked."

"Except that she got shot," says Becky.

"Well, that's the thing," says Hester. "Welcome to America."

Welcome to America.

I was struck—not for the first time—how easy and confident the nurses were in describing their work and their lives. There were moments, to be sure, when they clammed up. There were times when I could feel myself being directed away from a particularly sensitive story. The Med, like any hospital,

Becky Laster

must make mistakes, and from time to time nurses would tell me stories of the times things went wrong.

It is a curious process, being a stranger when others open up to you. You feel an immediate responsibility for the information. You hold it in trust and must use it carefully. And those moments of revelation can come in the most unexpected ways.

Most prosaically, perhaps, you learn something because you happen to be in the right place at the right time. Sometimes you learn by digging. Sometimes the endless process of comparing your notes against the official records produces an anomaly or a likely avenue of inquiry. Mostly you learn by smiling and listening. But just occasionally, on a journey like this, people talk to you precisely because you are a stranger far removed from the normal pressures of their life and their work. They talk to you because you carry no baggage. You have no rights in the matter, and you will not talk back.

There is one nurse I didn't get to know as well as I would have liked. Early on in my research we spoke briefly. She was interested in this book and seemed to have much to contribute. She had a clear-eyed view of the possibilities and limitations of nursing. She had a pleasingly sardonic take on the "We are all angels" view that some nurses hold. But she was not down on the profession. She had been a nurse for twenty years and saw no reason why she would not be a nurse for as many years to come. She had saved some people's lives, and seen others slip through her fingers. And she seemed to understand that nursing—that being a nurse—was a process, just as life is a process. Not for her the millennial rhetoric of improvement targets and budget savings. She embodied what I had come to understand nursing to be. She had even coined a Clintonesque phrase for it: "It's about people, stupid."

But then she disappeared from view for a while. Whenever I went by her department, she wasn't there. When I asked, other nurses preferred not to answer the question. I didn't think much of it, but on the off chance I sent her an e-mail, thinking perhaps she was on vacation.

Her reply came the same day.

"I wasn't at the Med last week," she wrote. "Trust me. I would have been delighted to have spent time with you rather than to have lived in my own surreal life this past week. Unfortunately my husband committed suicide. He shot himself in the head."

Even now, far away from Memphis and several months later, I can remember the numbing shock of reading those words.

The story gets worse.

"I was at the trauma center when I got the news—in the OR aggressively keeping a poor Oriental store owner alive while the surgeons patched up the many gunshot wounds that were inflicted on this man when he was robbed that day. I got the news that my husband killed himself. Suddenly I was living on the other side of these patients' lives. I was the family member who has been given the bad news of one of these tragic events. I found myself angry, screaming obscenities until I was out of air. Then I collapsed and wept. I felt the despair I had witnessed all too frequently. I felt the pain and confusion of losing a loved one here at the Med. I don't mind saying, I don't like being the family member who has to receive this kind of bad news. I'd much rather be on the other side, be one of the miracle workers. . . .

"There were no medical miracles that day," she went on. "Not for me. My husband of fifteen years was dead. But I have been overwhelmed with gratitude by the enormous support of the people of the Med. I have received so many blessings from them . . . in the form of plants and flowers, food, visits, phone calls, prayers and even a fistful of money from the many special people I work with. Here at the Med—*E Pluribus Unum*. Out of many, we are one."

A Kind of Crisis

THE REGIONAL MEDICAL CENTER at Memphis is a typical big-city hospital—and yet it is not typical. It is a special place in a specific town. It comes from a particular history, and that history is written into its patient load and staffing profiles.

And yet just as clearly it is representative of something. The debates over funding that occur at the Med are the same debates that happen across the country. The stories of the trauma ward—the stories of personal violence, of lives saved and lives lost—are a peculiarly American story. It is a kind of morality play in which the players are condemned to repeat the mistakes of the past, not because they do not understand that they are mistakes, but for want of any alternative. In chronicling the events at the Med over the course of a year I am struck by a polarity of possible understandings. Those who must necessarily grapple with the daily difficulties of running a major hospital—or working in a major hospital—must necessarily focus on short-term needs. Will we have enough money for tomorrow, for this month? Next year must—necessarily—take care of itself.

And yet to the outsider, the story is remarkably constant. Month after month, year after year, the administrative departments of the hospital produce figures that tell the story. Of those who come to the doors of the trauma unit, about 6 percent have injuries so bad that their lives cannot be saved. That's one hundred and something each year, a couple every week. In Trauma 70 percent of the patients are male, 50 percent are black. The average age is thirty-seven. One-third are self-pay, which, as any nurse will tell you, means no-pay. Only one-quarter have full insurance and there will therefore "always" be a budget deficit, a deficit that needs to be made up from public funds.

Trauma is only part of it; the patterns get repeated in all the Med's "centers of excellence," and in the "ordinary wards" as well.

At the Rout Newborn Center, for example, the nurses are part of a system that delivers extraordinary levels of care to a varied but constant number of patients. About 4,500 babies are born at the Med each year. Eighty percent of the mothers are African-American; only 12 percent are Caucasian. Half of the babies are vaginal deliveries without complications. Perhaps 10 percent are C-sections without complications. But a very large number—40 percent—need the kind of support and intervention that only a major hospital can provide. Many are very young mothers. The average age is twenty-three and a bit.

Their problems are the Med's problems. Their successes, the Med's successes. In the course of many visits to the Med I interviewed perhaps thirty nurses and spoke informally with many

more. There were complaints, but they were few. Dr. Steinhauer was right when he said that what nurses care about
most—assuming there is pay parity with other hospitals—is
whether there are enough of them to deliver the care they need
to deliver. Almost all the complaints I heard were about staffing
levels.

"It's not right," was one typical remark, "when you have patients asking if you're the only one working today."

"I haven't been able to eat today," said another in the
birthing unit. "No time."

Steinhauer was right, too, when he anticipated that nurses
more or less take it on faith that "something will turn up" to
cure the Med's financial ills. It was true last year, and the year
before, and the year before that. "There will always have to be
a public sector," Dr. Steinhauer said. "The Med ain't ever gonna
change," Dennis-who-lost-an-arm-and-a-leg told me. "The
Med has been like that for a hundred years. It's gonna be like
that a hundred years from now. And I'll tell you why. Because
it has to be. The Med has to take anyone who comes to its door,
and anyone who comes to its door don't always have the money
to pay."

"They can't afford to close us down," went the mantra.
"Where would all these people go?" And for another year they
were right. The Med, which the Memphis *Commercial Appeal*
was reporting as "on the precipice of ruin" on June 22, was alive
and well on July 4. And it was still there when I visited in October. But for how long?

A newly qualified nurse arriving at the Med will be put
through an orientation program. Her—or his—first task will

be to work through the orientation manual. On the first page she is greeted by a message from the director of training and development. "Hello," it reads. "We welcome you to this learning adventure."

To characterize working at the Med as an "adventure" is, in one sense, completely correct. The administration has, on the whole, a positive and engaged relationship with its workforce. There is a tangible sense of "We're all in this together," in this vibrant, beautiful, human institution. In another sense, however, it seems to me to miss the point. The essence of the idea of adventure is that there is progress, that things change and move forward. But as you read the hospital's caseload year on year, and as the endless wrangles over funding that have dogged the hospital since its beginning repeat themselves, "progress" seems a distant idea.

And yet, for all that, things change. Medical technology advances. New pharmaceuticals enter the marketplace. Patients who once would have been dead are now critical and the critical are stable. And nurses are better paid and better qualified. In some circles this might be considered progress. But over the year I spent visiting the Med I became aware that nurses judge themselves by different standards. Some came to the Med for the money—but the profession is not about money. Some came because the Med has always been part of their lives. But it is not about that. Some came because they want to help. But it is not really about that.

It seems to me in reading the testimony I have collated and in assessing the stories of the Med that this is really a narrative of belonging. The nurses at the Med feel they belong and they belong to something quintessentially human, which is to say an institution that is fractured, dispersed, incoherent and strange— but one that is also dynamic, changing and always open to the improvisations and needs of its users.

But it seems to me also that in belonging it is the nurses' lot to discover for themselves another, more oppressive, American truth: that to work in the contested arena of public service is to be part of a system in which all solutions are temporary and only the crisis is permanent.

Acknowledgments

There are no words to express my gratitude to the many nurses, doctors and administrators who spoke so freely while I was working on this book. Many are named in the text; many more are not. My thanks to them all. I am especially grateful to those who read the text and offered their comments and insights. Any errors that remain are entirely my own.

I am more grateful than I can say to Dr. Bruce Steinhauer and his executive team, who opened the doors to the Med and let me in.

I also want to thank my agent, Isobel Dixon, and my editor, Sara Carder, without whom this book would have been so much poorer.